The Mourning Road to Thanksgiving

The Mourning Road to Thanksgiving

by

Larry Spotted Crow Mann

CrowStorm Publishing 2016©

Acknowledgments

With deep gratitude, I want to thank all the readers for supporting this book. I must say it was a great delight and honor to bring this story to life. Thank you to my cousin, Nanci Race, for taking time to help with the editing; I profoundly appreciate it. Thank you, Tom Lusted for giving it the once over. Tom, you have great insight into story and scene. You were a great help. Thank you to the University of New Hampshire, Professor Siobhan Senier, for introducing me to Tom and all the wonderful work you do. Thank you to a special and dear friend, Nicole Sterling. Thank you for your dedication and commitment in helping with the final edits. And of course, helping me learn more things about Bruce Lee.

I want to thank the brilliant professors of UMass Amherst, Joyce Vincent and Ron Wellborn, for always giving me encouragement, support, and sharing their own wisdom as amazing writers and poets. A warm thank you to Professor, and good friend, Lisa Brooks. She also happens to be an awesome writer, historian, and a great help in all those fine details.

Thank you to all my Nipmuc folks for your support, as well as my large family in Québec. To my grandparents, who have crossed over to the Spirit World – Gladys, Benjamin, and Irene – thank you for the dreams. To my mom, Caroline, thank you for your overwhelming enthusiasm and support. And my dad, who unfortunately, I never had the chance to share with in this life, but yet, we are still a part of each other and maybe one day we will have that time we never had. Love you all!

To my sister, Juaquina, and my three brothers, Troy, Charles and Angel, through the good times, and not so good times, it's still has been wonderful to grow up with you. Thanks for always being there, love you guys. To all my aunts, uncles, cousins, nieces, and nephews – Love you all – thank you!

To all my children, Manixit, Mattawamp- Nantai, Mattonas-Anoki.

Of course, thank you, Mattonas– Anoki, for providing your face for the cover photo and Mayoke Photography for taking such a great shot.

And to all the First Nations people throughout United States, Canada and South America, I hope through my work that I have in some way carried your laughter, tears, joy, and pain so that the world may know and understand just a little bit more about who we are and show that all of us, as Human Beings, have a common bond. Kuttabatamish (Thank you very much).

Foreword

This novel does everything a good story is supposed to do. It made me stop reading at various moments to challenge my ideas and knowledge base, reflect, wonder, cry, and laugh. I thought about the characters even when I wasn't actively engrossed in the text.

My first thought when I finished the story was how necessary and important this book is on so many levels for so many people. As a reading specialist, I have seen more and more great books in schools that tell the stories of history from the Indigenous perspective -- written by Native Americans.

Yet, there are not as many books where young people can read about a character who is not only Native American but who is living in today's society and sharing his perspective on life -- not just in historical terms but in everyday living. As a teacher, I can only speak on how this book can remind readers (or, in some sad cases) inform for the first time, that Native peoples are very much here and have very important stories to share.

It is time for students in our schools (and people old and young in our society) to have these stories as a regular part of our learning, living, and engaging in our humanity.

This book is excellent. I want it in the hands of every teenager. We have needed this story in print for a very long time. - Karen Smith, Literacy Specialist

Historical Background

"In the beginning of all things, they say we Nipmuc started out as Sky Beings, without form, living with Manitoo in the vast darkness. Out of the darkness, Manitoo fashioned Mishe-Toonupasug (Great Turtle) as a symbol of his wisdom, patience, and old age. From the sweat of Manitoo's hands, he formed an enormous ball of water to be the home for the Turtle.

In the water, he made all sorts of life, some for the Turtle to feed on. As Mishe-Toonupasug became larger and larger, her back rose above the surface. As it rose, she brought up on her back the sands and stones from the bottom. This created the First Island. Our home— Turtle Island..."

This excerpt, from a Nipmuc Creation Story, illustrates Native American existence in North America thousands of years even before Europeans knew they were there. Archeological evidence across the continent, some dating back over twenty thousand years confirms this.

The Nipmucs are the original people of Worcester County, much of central New England, and beyond, stretching from Southern New Hampshire to Springfield, Massachusetts, and down into Northern Connecticut and Rhode Island. They lived in domed-style homes called Wetus' and also a larger style structure called a 'Longhouse.'

The people lived in over thirty villages throughout the area such as Wabaquasset, Quinnebaug, Quaboag, and Wachusett. Their economic and subsistence cycles consisted of hunting, gathering, planting, and harvesting in their seasons and trade. These villages were linked together by kinship ties, alliances, and common enemies. They were amongst the various Algonquian Speaking Tribes of New England that shared in a vast network of cultural exchange and trade that spanned hundreds of miles in every direction.

Over six hundred years before the Mayflower landed in Plymouth Harbor, the Norse (Icelandic/Norwegian) explorer Leif Eriksson had already visited the Indians of New England. By the 1500s, there were also the Portuguese Gasper and Miguel Corte Real, Esteven Gomez of Spain, Italian adventurer Giovanni de Verrazano, and many others (*Indian New England before the Mayflower*: Russell, 1980). In 1604, Samuel de Champlain would also make his voyage through New England. Many of these explorers had come to take part in the lucrative fur and timber trade, seek treasures, or take the Natives captive and sell them into slavery. However, for the most part, none of them intended to stay.

What they did leave behind were diseases like smallpox, measles, and tuberculosis. These illnesses were unknown whereby the people had no immunity. Indians died horrible deaths by the thousands. Upwards of eighty percent of the population had been wiped out due to these epidemics. For centuries, the Tribes of New England functioned in a balance of power, or reciprocity, that sustained an amicable way of life. This was not only practical, but was also in accord with their intrinsic relationship to the land around them: Never take more than you need and anything that is removed from nature must be replaced in kind.

If things did seem to fall out of balance – as indicated by a sudden loss or life or a shortage of food – ceremonies would be held to bring back harmony. A 'Giveaway' would be one ritual to take place that included singing and freely giving away items to family and friends. This ceremony could be used for many occasions but its main purpose was to restore stability within a person or the entire community. Another important gathering would be the Strawberry Moon Ceremony. This takes place each year in June. This ritual has to do with forgiveness and letting go of past grievances between family, friends and even enemies. This event is always accompanied by the ancient legend that speaks of why the strawberry is shaped like a heart and how it brought love in place of strife.

Massasoit was Grand Chief of the Pokanoket Tribe in the early 1600s. His main homeland was located near Bristol, Rhode Island. However, he had held great authority that stretched throughout the region. By the time the Pilgrims landed in 1620, the Indians of New England had already suffered at least two waves of devastating blights. The sudden and massive deaths led not only to a chaotic imbalance, but of doubt of their future existence as a people. Massasoit's leadership had been weakened and other Chiefs throughout the area stood to challenge or take over his authority.

When the 102, weak and weary, passengers aboard the Mayflower arrived in late 1620, they were in dire condition. What the Indians found odd about these people is that unlike the other European explorers, they planned to stay. Almost half of the Pilgrims didn't survive the first winter.

Massasoit had them under constant surveillance as he decided what to do. The Pilgrims were observed stealing stores of corn, looting, and desecrating graves. His first thought was to have them destroyed, but he reconsidered. Given his Tribe's weakened state, he deduced that these 'Whites' could become valuable allies against his enemies.

On March 22, 1621, a treaty of mutual respect and protection was drawn up between the Pilgrims and the Pokanoket Tribe. Massasoit and his people lent much support to these first settlers by teaching them how to farm, hunt, and fish. Also, they informed the Pilgrims of other Tribes and places to avoid.

The so-called First Thanksgiving was nothing like we have been taught in school. Firstly, the Pilgrims didn't refer to the gathering as

Thanksgiving, but more of an English harvest festival (*Mayflower*: Philbrick, 2006).

The Indians were not invited to the feast; they just showed up. One of the activities the Pilgrims held during this celebration was to practice their musket fire. Massasoit overheard the shooting and thought his newfound allies were in trouble. He came with 90 of his warriors to check the situation. Once he realized there was no danger, his men caught some deer and joined in on the banquet.

There was no sitting around a table. Most of them stood or sat on the ground near a fire. The English were also careful to keep their woman away from Indians. For the most part, the meal was a segregated event. Nonetheless, this mutual arrangement of peace seemed to work out for both parties.

Tranquility and respect did not endure long. As waves of Europeans began to settle in the Northeast, the insatiable appetite for animal pelts, timber, and land put a further strain on the Tribes. Indians had to find a new way to survive by adapting the English style of commerce.

The Pequot Indians of Southern Connecticut came to understand the value and leverage of taking up this trade and caught on rapidly. They became one of the most lucrative Tribes by dominating the fur trade.

A Sacred and important item, to all the Tribes, was Wampum. It was beads carved from the quahog shell used to create belts of information and sacred stories. Wampum was used as currency between the Tribes and English, but what became more common and widespread was the trade of alcohol brought by the English. Indians had never had alcohol and had a low tolerance for its effect. Indians were systematically cheated out of land, furs, and wampum while under the influence. Alcoholism and death from its cause was rampant amongst the Tribes.

The English wanted to put an end to its Pequot competition for furs and other goods. They also feared the Tribes' growing strength in fighting warriors. Unable to get rid of them with alcohol and trinkets, they led a preemptive attack.

In 1637, the English with the aid of allied Indians led an assault on the Pequot Mystic Fort. They surrounded the village and set it ablaze. Hundreds of men, women, and children were burned alive.

Governor William Bradford of Plymouth described the event: "It was a fearful sight to see them thus frying in the fryer, and the streams of blood quenching the same, and horrible was the stench and scent thereof; but the victory seemed a sweet sacrifice and we the Puritans gave the prayers thereof to God, who had wrought so wonderfully for us, thus to enclose our enemies in their hands and give us so speedy a victory over so proud and insulting an enemy (*Mayflower*: Philbrick, 2006)."

After this destruction, the English passed a law that any surviving Pequots would never be allowed to return home or call themselves Pequots again.

The first official "Day of Thanksgiving" was proclaimed in 1637 by Governor Winthrop in commemoration of the massacre of the Pequots:

"The 12th of the 8th m. was ordered to bee kept a day of publicke thanksgiving to God for his great m'cies in subdewing the Pecoits, bringing the soldiers in safety, the successe of the conference, & good news from Germany (Nathaniel Shurtleff, ed. *Records of the Governor and Company of the Massachusetts Bay in New England, Vol I.* Boston, 1853. p. 204)."

In the coming years, various English colonies took part in such feasts of Thanksgiving, but it wouldn't be until 1863 that the Country, as a whole, would have this as an official holiday.

It was turmoil heaped on agony for the Tribes when the Puritans forced Christianity upon them. The English believed the Indians were in league with devils and witches and must be converted or destroyed. This was left up to the Minster John Elliot. In the 1640s, he set up 'praying towns.' These were the first Reservations. Indians were forced to give up their culture, land, accept Christ, and live in a confined area. The other objective was to make room for new English settlements. They were not allowed to leave the praying towns under penalty of death. Indians who refused Christianity were under constant threat and had to push further inland.

The respect and fidelity the English first showed Massasoit had eroded. Bartering with them became extremely difficult for Massasoit. He witnessed the strength of his people dwindle and the English "sprouting up everywhere like leaves on a tree." The old Chief painfully observed his land being usurped and his people being subjugated and losing their way of life.

During the late 1650s, Massasoit permanently left Pokanoket and moved to the Nipmuc village of Quaboag (Indians of Nipmuck Country: Connole 2001). This area was located around in what is now Brookfield, Massachusetts. He changed his name to Ousamequin, which means Yellow Feather. He became one of the Grand Chiefs of the Nipmuc Tribe of Quaboag.

Massasoit's (Ousamequin's) two sons, Wamsutta (aka Alexander) and Metacom (aka Phillip), were left to take over the Pokanoket Tribe. Alexander died of mysterious causes; most believe he was poisoned. This left his brother Phillip to take over; when he did, he became known as King Phillip.

A society, culture, and way of life that endured even through the last ice age, was decimated and on the verge of extinction within a span of fifty-five years after the landing of the Mayflower. The Pilgrims came to America seeking independence and religious freedom but were not willing to extend these same human rights to the Natives who first welcomed them.

The Indians of the region had had enough and formed a powerful alliance to fight for their survival. In 1675, one of the bloodiest wars on American soil erupted across the land, and came to be known as the King Phillip's War.

Nipmuc Indians joined by the thousands. One Nipmuc Chief in particular, named Mattawamp, was said to be the most brilliant military leader of the war. He commanded some of the most smashing victories of the war: Wheeler's Surprise, Brookfield, Bloody Brook, and New Braintree (*King Phillips War*: Schultz & Tougais 1999).

As the battle spread, the English shut down the praying towns. Even though these 'praying town Indians' remained loyal to the English and never took up arms, they were forcibly interned to Deer Island. The majority of them froze and starved to death. Some were sold into slavery in the West Indies.

During the King Phillip's War, there was a massive loss of life and devastation on both sides. The Native warriors were winning the battles but losing the war. The English were able to replenish supplies of weapons, soldiers, and recruit desperate Indian allies, while the warriors fighting for freedom had to stay on the move. Hunger, cold, and the inability to replace dead men took its toll. When King Phillip was killed and beheaded, this further demoralized the warriors. The same fate would come of Mattawamp and many others.

By the end of 1676, with the major Native leaders killed, many asked for a truce agreement and surrendered. A mass number turned themselves in under this truce agreement only to be executed or shipped into slavery. Hundreds – perhaps thousands took part in a diaspora and headed into Canada. By the 1700s, disease, loss of land, discrimination, poverty, and the ills of rampant alcoholism pushed the remaining Indians to the edge of society. Indians of New England drifted on the precipice of obscurity and became a thing of the past in the minds of Americans. The Nipmuc homeland, which once spanned over 2000 square miles, had been reduced to five acres.

In 1861, Indian Agent for Massachusetts, John Milton Earle, set out to check the condition of the Indians and enumerate them. This list became known as the "Earle Report." Although incomplete, the Earle Report is one of the methods that the Indians of Massachusetts utilize to trace their lineage.

Earle noted that some of the Indians were living on small Reservations, others in the backwoods of small towns as paupers. Many turned to their cultural knowledge to survive: They went door to door to White households selling handmade Indian baskets, brooms, wood carvings, and other crafts.

Even though many Indians married into the White and African American race, they carried within them their culture and traditional knowledge. Being Indian was more about a historical bloodline, living within their Native tradition, and the stories that were passed down rather than an outward appearance. The individuals who have the hereditary roots don't have any doubts about who they are.

However, this led to a major and perplexing question of Indian identity that started with a so-called blood quantum. Measuring one's blood quantum to certify whether they were Indian or not was a practice that originated with the United States Government. This was a way for the Government to usurp Tribal lands and Indian rights if a person was found to be 'mixed' or not have 'enough Indian blood.'

Ironically, at the same time, the United States applied the 'one drop rule' to African Americans. This meant that any person, any time in their history who had even the smallest amount of African American ancestry, were deemed Black. Historically, Indians always adopted people into their nations and it had nothing to do with a blood quantum. But eventually, many Tribal nations began to use this method to the detriment of many Indian people. Other requirements, such as whether a person speaks their Tribal language grew up on the Reservation; and whether their bloodline is maternal or paternal could play a factor in Tribal membership. Some Tribes have not taken the path of blood quantum and determine membership through genealogical descendancy. Whether it's the Federal Government, State, or Indian-to-Indian, the matter of who is an Indian person, and how they are defined remains to be one of the most controversial and hot-button topics for Tribes across the United States and Canada.

Indians across the country would struggle with poverty, discrimination, loss of lands, and removals to boarding schools into the next century. Native Americans were wards of the State and were not United States Citizens until 1924. Freedom of religion for Native Americans would not come until 1978.

First through theatrical plays, then on the movie screen, Indians became a living caricature. They became mascots and mythologies as there was very little, if any, information on whom the real Indian people are. For many years, due to the lack of information and research; the school classroom was also a fertile ground for stereotypes to be firmly stamped in our minds. Inculcated versions of Indians and Pilgrims smiling across a harmonious dinner table became the bedrock of misinformation.

But, as before, Indian people came together to rebuild and try to restore what was taken away. There was a new social conscious on the rise throughout the world. Much like the Civil Rights Movement in the 1960s, The American Indian Movement (AIM) of the 1970s came to be the rallying call for Indian people from coast to coast. They fought for social justice, honoring the treaties, and the return of Tribal lands. Indians and White allies joined in marches and protests to bring a new-found voice and awareness to the struggles of Indian people. Tribal pride was growing again. Indians from every state were joining groups, strengthening their Tribes, and rallying for rights and respect.

For some, the Thanksgiving holiday itself became the symbol of centuries of genocide and oppression. In 1970, the "National Day of Mourning" was created in opposition to the Thanksgiving holiday by the Wampanoag, Wamsutta Frank James, and the United American Indians of New England. It is held every year in Plymouth, Massachusetts on the same day as Thanksgiving. It has become an International event with Tribal leaders and people from around the world who come to participate.

The saga of Native Americans is rich, complex, and full of wonders yet to be explored. The Mourning Road to Thanksgiving reveals a new path into this dynamic journey in a groundbreaking story that must be told.

This modern tale is a work of historical fiction but is entrenched in the actual history, tradition, and lives of Indians of the past and present. It will beckon all your emotions in a novel that you will want to read again and again.

The Mourning Road to Thanksgiving should be read by everyone, from grade nine and up. This book will serve as a vital resource and provide the catalyst for other Native American topics yet to be thoroughly explored.

Note: The terms Native American, First Nations, or Indian are used interchangeably.

Table of Contents

Preface

How can a holiday stir up thoughts of cheer, warmth, and celebration in some, while reminding others of a painful and dark past? For millions of Americans, primarily Native Americans, that is a lingering question that poses itself every last Thursday of November. I have been asked through the years, "Do Native Americans celebrate Thanksgiving and how do they feel about it?" It's not a simple response and, certainly, the answer is far more complicated than one could imagine. It's not because we don't like turkey, pie, and football. Native Americans always love a good feast. The conflict arises when we consider that the founding of this day of giving thanks for some was inextricably linked to an era of taking away from others. Not only stripped of life and land; but even the Voice of Native people would be controlled, contained, and filtered through a toxic narrative to bring forth devastating effects— even to this day.

Many are familiar with the story of the Mayflower landing at Plymouth Rock, the iconic breaking of bread between the "Indians and Pilgrims," and the legacy it birthed. The Mourning Road to Thanksgiving skillfully dismantles the accepted narrative by illuminating untold historical facts in a spectacular story that will change the way we appreciate this celebration, ourselves, and America.

In an epic saga carved from the real life events, we take you on an exploration of an American tradition like never before. With each turning page, you step deeper into the complex life and experiences of the First People of this land and how they've had to cope and adapt for centuries.

The Thanksgiving holiday is the main course where this rare taste of America gets served.

Neempau Stoneturtle is a 40-year-old Native American Nipmuc man haunted by the past and fighting to change the future. He believes the Thanksgiving holiday should officially be a day of mourning. He wants to stop the celebration and lofty narrative portrayed by all of America, but he must convince his sister first. His parents, who have long been deceased, were deeply involved in the Native American Civil Rights Movement. Neempau has tried to carry on that legacy but his sister, Keenah, has taken a more mainstream path. Neempau will encounter many unforeseen obstacles on his journey including coming to terms with his own past.

This riveting tale challenges the narrative and conceptions we have of American history and exposes the untold stories and lingering scars of our past. As equally important, this is a story for our generation. It takes us bravely forward to an understanding and awareness of each other like never before. From laughter to tears, this novel will inspire you and reveal the endless possibilities when we open our hearts.

All My Relations

Chapter 1

Nequt

"Ugh! They warned me about you. I've got a good notion to rip out all that wild hair! You are not going to ruin this class's Thanksgiving Day activities with your nonsense. Now, you pick up that Indian hat you threw on the floor, or you'll spend the rest of the fourth grade in the corner, buster!"

"Bu-but, Ms. Nelson, my dad told me we're not supposed to wear pretend feathers. He-he said it's not respectful."

Ms. Nelson unclenched her thin, pale hands that were entrenched in the boy's hair, took a step back, and bent her upper body forward with her hands in a praying position. Her eyes cut into him.

"Hmm... I think your dad is just a little bit confused," she stated with a condescending tone. She sucked her teeth. "You see, we're here to honor your heritage. We have the other kids playing the Pilgrims to honor their great heritage and the founding of our wonderful nation. And, of course, your people helped a little. Don't you want to honor the Nipmucs? Besides, all the other classes will be green with envy because we have a real Indian in our Thanksgiving Day activities."

The teacher picked up the paper 'Indian feather' hat and secured it back on the boy's head.

"There! You look handsome," she declared, her eyes blinking quickly.

With his hand trembling and tears beginning to swell in his eyes, the child once again ripped off the paper feather hat and threw it on the floor.

Ms. Nelson's eyebrows became tight, her cheeks puffed up as her mouth shrank. Her screeching voice ejected from her mouth like an ear-piercing siren, "How dare you!?"

She clutched the boy by the arm as tight as she could, and then shook his thin body. His head jolted and his two long braids flailed and whipped as if caught in a vicious storm. Her nose seemed to bend a little when she pressed her face into the side of his head. The odor of her morning coffee, boiled eggs, and Viceroys came rushing into the student's nose as she shouted "That's it, buster! I'm done with you! You're going to get it!"

~~~

"Whaaaaah!"

The harsh cry of the infant four seats to the rear wakened him. He lifted his head off the bus window. With the impression of the window still on his cheek, he rubbed his eyes, shook his head and glanced around.

It was early morning, one week before Thanksgiving and forty-year-old Neempau Stoneturtle was on a bus heading to his younger sister, Keenah's, house; she lived an hour from the Nipmuc Reserve in Massachusetts.

Neempau had that kind of look that could have been in a sporting or rock-and-roll magazine. The scar over his left eyebrow gave an added look of adventure to his smooth round face. Years of demanding work have left him in good physical condition.

Neempau peered over the seat in the direction of the wailing child. He noticed the infant's mother calming her baby with her breast milk. His dark brown eyes made contact with the nursing mother's blue. She casually smiled at the half-hidden face and nodded in his direction. He blushed with embarrassment and returned a timid smile. He slowly twisted back around and sank in his chair.

He redirected his sight out the window at the expanse of pines, hemlocks, and rolling mountains, as the bus trekked Eastbound on I-90 towards Massachusetts.

Neempau slid his hands down his two long braids, as if trying to smooth the frizziness. The braids rested across his broad chest and over his faded thick-denim coat, one of them over the round black and white patch above his left pocket that read, "Stop the Keystone Pipeline." On the opposite side, there was a hand-stitched emblem of the Nipmuc Medicine Wheel.

Neempau had not seen his sister Keenah for over ten years. He had dropped out of high school in the 10th grade and got his GED. Other than returning briefly for important ceremonies such as funerals, Neempau had been living away from Nipmuc lands since his early 20s.

He took a job as an ironworker and went wherever he could get an assignment. Throughout his life, he earnestly tried to uphold the Nipmuc traditions taught to him by his parents: Water Drum songs, the Corn Dance, Strawberry, and Planting Moon Ceremonies. These, along with other traditional events, carry a strong emphasis on connecting to the spirit world, honoring Mother Earth, and the reciprocity of the community.

During his travelling years, wherever it might be, he would go to the nearest Reserve and partake in ceremony with the local Tribe, especially when up North. The ceremonial Longhouse was where he would partake in social and Water Drum songs with close friends. These were the ways Neempau and Keenah were raised: honor their culture, never forget who they are, and most importantly, fight for their rights and land.

Neempau's dad passed away shortly after he completed his training as an ironworker, and his mom died several years later. Their parents were part of several Indian Civil Rights Movements of their time: marches in DC, protests against corporations trying to build on Indian land, protecting Indian burial sites, water and fishing rights, anti-police brutality, and discrimination protests. In the early 1970s, they were labeled 'communists' and 'anti-American militants' by the State for their activist involvement. This tag also led them to be harassed or jailed at times.

From toddlers to teens, Neempau and Keenah were there through it all. Every conversation they heard around the house concerned political, social, spiritual, and economic rights for Native Americans. There was always a house full of Indians; some preparing for protests while others were conducting ceremonial sweat lodges and drum circles that went all night long. At a young age, Keenah and Neempau did not fully understand what was happening at the time, but those years left an indelible mark on their lives.

Their adolescent school life was very difficult. There was only a handful of Indians who attended their public school. They felt more like worms at a chicken dance than like students. Because he would get into scuffles with boys who pulled his long hair, called him a girl, and made fun of his name, Neempau learned how to fight at an early age.

Keenah was referred to as the 'Little Squaw' by a few classmates and even by some of her teachers. That was a term used to demean Native American women in early American films. At times, their

7

parents would have to go the school and demand that their children be treated with respect. It seemed that all the other children who attended the school had a place and did fit in.

On one particular day, Neempau was coming home from school with scrapes and bruises. He had gotten into a fight in the cafeteria with two boys. They repeatedly called him 'sneaky redskin' and warned all the other children in the lunch room, "Hey everybody, watch out! Use your lunch tray as a shield! Neempau's gonna scalp us!"

All the boys were reprimanded and sent home. The school principal later discovered that the two kids were watching an old movie the night before, 'The Charge at Feather River,' and were simply repeating what they observed.

When Neempau arrived at home, hair and face a mess, and torn shirt he said, "Mom! Dad! You told me we were here in this Country first, right? Then why are we always the ones nobody understands? Treated like outsiders?"

His mother began to tenderly wipe the dried blood from under his nose. She patted his head and looked sincerely at him.

"I know, baby, I know," she said. "*This* is what me and your dad are fighting for. So that when you grow up, you will never have to see this type of ignorance again."

Neempau's father took a deep breath before speaking, as if he were a overheated car, "I will talk with the principal tomorrow, but tonight, we are all going out to have some burgers and ice cream. Don't worry about it, my little Chief; everything's gonna be ok."

The holidays were some of the most awkward times for the siblings. They never celebrated Thanksgiving because they were taught that that was a day for mourning. Instead of a big fancy feast around a table, they drummed and danced as they partook in their

Tribe's Harvest Moon Ceremony. This was the annual ceremony and feast that coincided with giving thanks for the Fall Harvest. Honoring the Ancestors, Giveaways, and sharing traditional stories were also an important part of this ritual.

Some years, they took their large van and drove up to Plymouth, Massachusetts to contribute to the National Day of Mourning. This memorial was founded by members of the Wampanoag Tribe, but now serves as a beacon for indigenous people everywhere. Native Americans from New England and beyond participate in the event, along with hundreds (if not thousands,) of non-Natives who sympathize with Native American rights.

The National Day of Mourning would be filled with prayer, drumming, marches, and powerful speeches. Medicine Men, Clan Mothers, Chiefs, and Indian Activists from all over the North and South America would come to share about their nation and a hope for a better future for all.

Being there to protect, teach, and love their children were all-important. But the Stoneturtles also knew their calling went beyond their own family. The 70s and 80s saw many positive changes for Indian people because of people like them who made it their mission to stand up and fight to change the world.

Neempau made it his mission to carry on the legacy of his parents. However, Keenah's life took a different path. After she graduated from high school she went on to college to get her nursing degree. That's where she met and married her husband, George House, who was also Nipmuc. George was a by-the-book claims supervisor at an insurance company who lived a more 'mainstream' life with Keenah. They had two children – 17 year-old Silvia, and 14 year-old Robert.

Finally, after over a decade, Neempau was going to visit his sister Keenah and her family at their beautiful home. Next to Columbus

Day, Thanksgiving was Neempau's most despised holiday. Keenah, however, had been celebrating Thanksgiving with her family since she was married and had always invited her brother, but he's refused to come until now.

~~~

After settling in, Neempau reached into his backpack and pulled out his lunch. It was bannock bread filled with cranberries, nuts and bacon bits wrapped in foil. He took a quick breath as he stared at his snack. He gently touched along the edge of the wrapping as he slowly unraveled it. His thoughts were swept back to the moments before he set off on this bus trip.

"I made you some snacks, but don't eat it now. Save it for your trip. I'll wrap it for ya. Neempau, are you sure you're ready to go back this time?"

He stood at the doorway, gazing aimlessly out the small square window.

"Neempau? You told me going there burns you up inside."

"Huh- what?"

"Don't forget, the Ironworkers' Union may call you back for a job, you know. You gave them many years of hard work. I don't think that one time will—"

"No. I can't do that work anymore. You can donate all my books to your Tribal library."

"Is that your way of saying you're not coming back?"

His mouth opened but words failed to follow.

"The youth are going to miss all those Nipmuc legends you shared and *I'm* going to miss you, you know that," Gladys said. "I've gotten used to our 'sometimes-lover-sometimes-friend relationship.' I know it's the panic attacks and anxiety that keeps you from getting close. With my busy work schedule—"

"I don't have anxiety."

"Lots of people have it, Neempau, it's not like—"

"Gladys, I told you, I don't have anxiety."

"Well, whatever it is, it has been worse this last week."

She took a discomfited pause from preparing the meal, as if wishing to take back what she just said. Gladys walked over to Neempau, held his hands and said in a patient tone, "You're right. I'm sorry."

"You don't have to say sorry. It's ok, I appreciate all you do. But I'm alright. I'm going to miss everyone here too. It's nice to see the kids so eager to hear the stories. Take care of yourself, Gladys."

A couple of hours after Neempau had left, Gladys began to pack up his books in old soda crates. As she pulled 'God is Red' by Vine Deloria from the shelves, a letter fell to the floor. It was a notice from the court dated ten days prior, which read in part: "You are hereby notified that your final appeal has been denied."

~~~

Neempau had finished up his meal as the bus slowed down in the city of Worcester to make a stop. He gave a dismissive gaze to all the Thanksgiving signage posted throughout the city. He reflected back on how all this land used to belong to the Nipmuc. He pictured the beautiful Nipmuc village that once stood here long ago named Pakachoag, a large, healthy community of artists, builders, farmers, hunters, warriors, and Chiefs — a land where elders passed down ancient stories and traditions, and Medicine Men and Women relayed the knowledge of Earth Medicine. Here, children were taught at birth the inherent connection of all things in the universe, and that laughter was more precious than strict puritanical rules.

For thousands of years, as if rooted to the very earth itself, their sturdily-constructed *Wetus'* and long houses propagated alongside the bountiful lakes, sparkling rivers, rolling hills, and between the pines, oaks, and willow trees. Wolves were not, yet, hunted to near extinction. They traversed the valley in great multitudes like regal guardians keeping the land in balance. The sky above was clean, crisp, and bald eagles flourished.

Now it is littered with factories, buildings, cars, and pollution. Neempau wryly took notice of a massive 30-foot inflated pilgrim next to a used car dealer lot. The bloated pilgrim was holding a sign that said: "Don't Be a Turkey! Get Served 1st at Winslow's Fine Used Cars!"

He spotted a billboard up the road that depicted the First Thanksgiving, which caused him to shake his head in disgust. Neempau saw that the picture had the Indian men wearing Western plains-style feather bonnets on their heads – local Tribes do not wear those. Also, the Pilgrims towered over the Natives at the table – Eastern Woodland Indians are known for their height and were much taller than the gaunt first settlers.

Furthermore, the Native Americans were sporting extra-large smiles, as if coat hangers were stuck in their mouths. The message over the picture read: "Shop at Mayflowers – For A-Maize-Ingly Low Prices!"

The bus pulled into the terminal. Inside, people were bustling on and off the bus in their usual holiday fashion as they rushed to see loved ones, tried to catch sales, or head on vacation in this obnoxious surge of movement.

Neempau impatiently looked on as he sat there waiting for the bus to get moving. However, there was one last passenger to come aboard. But before he was seen, he was heard. Like an unforeseen tornado, the bus was rapidly bombarded with a distressed intonation.

"Thuh- song- you- sang- soo- sweetly- out- in- dah- cold- out-in- dah- cold -again!"

The uproar was coming from an African-American male in his late 60s. He was attempting to sing an old Frankie Lymon song, but he was way off key and slurring his words – the man was extremely inebriated. His worn down, withered face spoke of a hard life of drinking and perhaps suffering. His unkempt beard was completely white. His short, gray afro was partially hidden underneath his unclean, beat-up train engineer hat, that seemed to be barely staying on his head. His navy blue jacket resembled that of a mechanic and was torn under the left armpit. The coat also had blotches of dried blood and soil down the front right side. His red pants were faded and stained with some sort of sauce. His legs were as thin as pool sticks and appeared to be on backwards. One of his high-top sneaker shoe- laces was the end piece of a telephone cord.

As he swayed and wobbled down the aisle, his legs were too far out in front of him. His hands were flapping around as if he were a newly blind man feeling his way through a dark world. While the man was still proceeding down the aisle, the bus departed from the terminal.

The sudden movement caused the drunken gentleman to fall, face first, right into Neempau's lap. The old man's hat tumbled to the floor. The backside of his pants revealed part of his rear-end, and his back pocket held a pint of 6-dollar wine.

Neempau's large hands quickly gripped the man and sat him upright in the seat beside him. "Whoa-whoa! Are you okay?" asked Neempau.

The man's voice seemed to alternate from gravelly deep to high pitch. He was also trying to speak Spanish to Neempau: "Aaaah, p- perdón - Ah- -may- por- fav—"

After a little frustration he gave up his attempt and said, "I–I—I be fine, I be fine! P— Pa— Pass me my cap here."

Neempau sighed as he passed the hat.

The man continued on and said, "Hah! Thay— thay— thay— thank you much. Hah! I nee— needs that hat. This be my lucky hat." He laughed loudly.

Neempau looked at him with a quick annoyed smile but then grimaced, for by now his nose was taken prisoner by the arresting stench of stale alcohol and rancid body odor. To avoid the fumes, Neempau kept his face close to the window. Despite his endeavor for fresh air, the man wanted his attention.

"Say— say— say now. You know wh— why this be my lucky hat?"

Still looking out the window, Neempau took a deep breath. "No, I don't," he answered sharply.

The man responded in a loud and energetic voice, "Be— because it be the only thang keepin' my head together!"

The man started clapping and belly laughed, which caused others on the bus to shush him.

The man said to Neempau, "Oh— oh, my 'pology. My name be Willie James the III, and who you be?" Because of the man's rollercoaster, rapid speech, his name actually sounded like "Will-J."

Neempau turned to Willie and said in an irritated tone, "Um, yeah, hello. How ya doing? I'm Neempau Stoneturtle."

Willie James intensely stared at Neempau, his eyes crisscrossed for a moment as his head teetered slowly on his thin neck. This time it was Willie who turned away. His disheveled body curved toward the aisle as he wrinkled his lips.

He mumbled to himself "Ne— Neema— Neema? What da hell's a Neema?"

Willie broke into a robust laugh then harshly attempted his best Frankie Lymon again. This caused some of the other passengers to turn angrily back in their seats.

He reached in his back pocket, pulled out the bottle of wine and said to Neempau, "Ha— Happy Thanksgivin', Neena! Le— Le's drank to the Hollidaze! Le— let me give you uh drank!"

Neempau made a stop sign signal with his hand and replied, "No. I'm all set, thanks."

With a heavy burp and chuckle, Willie replied, "Hah, that be fine. Fine, Neena. That's just more for me" he chuckled. "Say now, where you be headin'?"

Following a short pause, Neempau answered, "I'm going to visit some family I have not seen in a while."

"Ah, now— now that be so nice. Just in time for Thanksgivin."

Neempau sat straight up and said, "What? You kiddin' me? Celebrate that nonsense? It's all lies. Nothing but a big profit-making machine based on lies – the White man's lies."

"All right, now. All-right! Don't go all h-h-hot tamale, Neeka! You— you folk have some other kind of siesta you celebrates, I know."

"Umm, I think you mean fiesta, but—"

"Now, now! Look here: Don't you make no never mind about no White folks and them lies, cause see here - the White man gonna do and say whatever he got to. See here. He ain't lying to you, boy. That's called the law." Willie's eyes became wider for a moment, "So don't you pay no attention to that foolishness. You get yourself, an edu-macation; beat him at his own game—see here?"

Even though Neempau grinned in light of the admonitions, he did lower his head in affirmation. Willie's intoxicated eyes vigilantly zoomed in and out on Neempau's response as his head swayed side to side.

Once he realized his tutelage was getting through, his body jerked forward and he said, "Hah! See— see you gots to listen at ole Willie. I sets ya straight!"

Neempau chuckled.

"Well, I hopes you have a mighty fine trip with your family."

"Thanks. So where are you going, to see some family too?" asked Neempau.

"No, no! Nothin' like that boy, nothin' like that. I is headin' down to the new shelter in Morristown. Veterans Affairs Office got me a bed over there. It's fixin' to gets real cold out here."

Neempau somberly glanced to the bus floor, looking as if he was about to say something. Instead, he turned his gaze back out the window.

Willie glanced over and examined Neempau- "Dog gone, boy, how long it took you to grow that hair? And- and what's that you wearin' on your neck there?"

"This is a wampum necklace, carved from quahog shells. Just like my earrings. See the purple ones? They are more valuable."

"Shells? Huh, alright, nice, I'm a get me one."

"And the last time I cut my hair—" Neempau stopped in mid sentence.

Willie had abruptly tipped his bottle of wine vertically up to his mouth and was swallowing in large gulps. The guzzling sounds had drowned out Neempau's words. Willie wiped the spillage from his beard with the back of his left forearm, released a monstrous belch, and declared, "This be some good, good stuff. You sure you don'ts want none?"

"I appreciate the offer, but no, thanks."

16

Willie buckled in his seat then leaned closer to Neempau, which brought in a more potent, adverse odor of body and booze.

Willie held the bottle of wine close to Neempau's head and said, "Wha— Wha's wrong? This be some good wine. But see here, I used to be a gin man. Hah! They use to call Ol' Willie-J 'Baby Maka Gin Man' hah!"

Willie roughly heaved his body to his feet, attempted to do a spin but nearly fell, saved by the seat rail that held him up. He began shaking and gyrating his hips while clapping and singing loudly: "I is the Gin Man! Gin Man! Gin Man, baby maka Gin Man!"

A passenger from near the front yelled out, "Hey! Shut up and sit down before I throw you off this bus!"

Willie snapped back, "Ah, why don't-cha go own somewhere? I— I— I— come up there in go upside your head! Throw Ol' Willie-J off the bus? Shoot! Thro— throw me off the bus? I is fixin' to pull a Rosa Parks on your behind! Throw me off the bus? Huh! B— better throw me a drank, dammit!"

As Willie continued yelling and bouncing in place, Neempau cut in and said in a calm voice, "Hey, hey, Willie. Why don't you just sit down? Take it easy."

Willie paused and gave Neempau a sour glance, but then said, "O— OK. I— I'll sit down. That duck plucker better be lucky!"

As Willie sat down he had one more thing to say, "You lucky Meeda's here to calm ole Willie down! Shoot! They use' to call me 'Voodoo on a Stick' back in Bunkie, Louisiana! I'll be the wizard that turns you into a gizzard!"

He continued to cynically peer toward the front of the bus. Then he leaned toward Neempau holding out the top of both hands.

He said, "Now look it that, boy. See that? My hands is black – like they supposed to be. But now watch this — watch this."

17

Willie flipped both hands over and revealed his palms and said, "Now see? See how Whites they is? You know why my palms be so white?"

Neempau was bewildered, but amused, and was not sure how to respond. Nonetheless, Willie gave his explanation. "My palms be so white 'cause of all those White folk I done smacked! Hah!"

Neempau shook his head, laughed, and said, "Willie, you're okay in my book."

Shortly afterward, Willie's attention was caught by a fast-food Mexican eatery the bus was going by.

He excitedly shouted to Neempau, "Hey! Hey there, Keemo! That be some good food up in there; yaw folks makes some good tacos!"

Neempau's cheer quickly diminished and he replied in a slightly louder voice while squeezing his teeth together, "Geez, man! Look it. My name is Neempau – Neempau. And I'm a Nipmuc Indian from right here in Massachusetts where we come from," he said, "I don't speak Spanish; I'm not a Mexican, Puerto Rican, Cuban, whatever. Now, come on – would you knock it off?"

Willie bobbed his head, again, and gruffly shouted, "W— Well, go back to Calcutta!"

Neempau became silent. He clenched his jaw and his eyes tensed as he looked toward Willie. However, despite his anger, a slight smile took over his face. Neempau chuckled and turned back to the window while Willie continued to mumble until he drifted to sleep.

Thirty minutes later, with Willie fast asleep on his shoulder, Neempau reached his destination. Neempau gently shifted Willie's head to the seat, reached overhead to get his black backpack, and began making his way off the bus. He stopped and turned back towards the passed-out Willie. He looked at him, pulled out a $20 and four, crinkled one-dollar bills from his wallet, and stuffed them inside Willie's top jacket pocket. Just as the bus driver yelled, "Last call!" Neempau made his exit.

Chapter 2

Neese

Neempau got off at the nearest bus stop to his sister's house which was still six miles away. He inhaled a deep breath to take in the crisp fall country air and perhaps to also ease his senses from the ripe smell of his fellow passenger. He tossed on his backpack and began his walk. As he made his journey down the road, he noticed many of the nice homes had their front doors decorated with dried 'Indian corn' and paper turkeys along with large pumpkins on the steps.

Neempau gazed at the holiday décor with vitriol and thought, 'Look at these idiots, celebrating their reign of genocide. I wonder if all these 'good Christians' will be forgiven for having their home covered in those Pagan deities? They love everything about the Indian, except the Indian.'

He approached a mailbox at the edge the road; it was decorated with a festive wooden turkey sporting a pilgrim hat. He noticed the turkey had that same extra-large grin the Indians had in that billboard sign back in Worcester.

Neempau locked eyes with the ornament – it seemed to stare back in a taunting and mocking fashion. He took a cautious look around and then, with a hard elbow check, knocked off the head of the wooden turkey and proceeded up the road.

Soon thereafter, a school bus pulled up just ahead to drop off some youths. The frolicking kids departed to the sound of "Happy Thanksgiving!" from the bus driver.

The students were quickly scattering in the direction of their homes, eager to start Thanksgiving vacation. Just as Neempau walked by the bus, the last child came barreling off, and bumped into him. It was a husky, White male with sandy brown hair who looked about eleven years old. He was wearing an Indian feather head dress cut out of paper.

As the boy's face collided into Neempau's ribs, the paper Indian feathers scratched against his chin and bottom lip. The boy simply looked up at Neempau with an innocent smile and said, "Excuse me, Happy Thanksgiving, Mister!"

Neempau awkwardly looked at the youth, not sure how to respond. He forced a smile and waved as he quickened his pace to get away. After about 40 yards, Neempau stopped and glanced back over his shoulder. A sudden and brisk autumn wind stirred his braids as it hurled maple leaves about his boots. Neempau tensely stared in the direction of the child, as if words were building up from deep inside, and about to erupt. Instead of speaking, he drifted into a haze of thought, as the sound of a crow's caw faded in the distance. He began to reflect on the stirring dream he had on the bus; that lingering dream and memory always stayed with him, like a dark cave holding the echoes of pain.

"Ugh! They warned me about you. I've got a good notion to rip out all that heathen hair! You are not going to ruin this class's Thanksgiving Day activities with your nonsense. Now, you pick up that Indian hat you threw on the floor, or you'll spend the rest of the 4th grade in the corner, buster!"

"Bu— but, Ms. Nelson, my dad told me that we're not supposed to wear pretend feathers. He—he said it's not respectful."

"I am your teacher! Your father," she said, "Is not here! This is your last warning!" As Ms. Nelson put the paper Indian feather hat on him, the tears began to flow from the shaking little boy.

Abruptly, 11 year-old Neempau removed it, only moments after she put it on. Ms. Nelson's pale thin face turned hot pink and her eyes closed in on Neempau. She swiftly grasped the boy by the arm and twisted while jolting his small body. She forcefully pressed her forehead into the side of his head while saying in a loud voice, "That's it, buster! I'm done with you! You're going to get it!"

His body whiplashed and jerked as she dragged him down the hall. Her voice became low and unnerving, "You think you're going to the corner? That's where the normal students go for discipline. You're not normal; you're a little wild Indian and you need to be locked away."

Neempau was heaved into the small and empty janitor's closet, which was located out of sight behind the coatroom.

Ms. Nelson declared, in a sharp tone, "Now, you will stay in here every day until you wear that hat. You can stay in there until the Spring if need be."

With a sudden and unforgiving slam, Neempau was cast into the dark.

Other voices and memories became interspersed within his childhood nightmare, swirling in his head like the blowing leaves.

"Get your hands off me! I know my rights!"

"It's your entire fault, Neempau!"

~~~

The sound of loud beep snapped Neempau out of reverie and freed him from those painful recollections. It was the horn from a brand new shiny black Mustang GT 500. It pulled up beside Neempau.

23

There was music blasting from the radio - Jerry Alfred & The Medicine Beat were singing their hit "Ney-A-Na."

The driver of the Mustang was Neempau's 35-year-old, fun-loving, and ostentatious cousin Martin Attuck Jr., better known as 'Wavy.' He'd been called Wavy since he was a youth because of his thick, black, curly hair, which he still had. Wavy had a healthy build, average height, and a lively brown complexion. His auburn eyes were adorned with fancy Aviator-style sunglasses. He had a gap between his front teeth, and his face was smooth, save for his small goatee.

That day he was wearing a red bandana across his forehead and his black locks fell to his shoulders, just barely touching his brown leather jacket. As his Mustang came to a stop, he turned the music down, leaned over the passenger seat, and looked above his sunglasses to get a better look at Neempau.

In a surprised, rolling voice, Wavy shouted "Whoooolee! Whooolee! Is that? Could it be? Neempau? My big Cuz, Neempau Stoneturtle?"

Wavy jumped out of the car, leaving his door open, and roared, "Ooooh, man! Give me a hug, Cousin!"

Wavy excitedly embraced him, while Neempau reciprocated the hug in a more reserved fashion. Wavy pulled back and squeezed Neempau by both shoulders and shouted, "Whooolee! It's you! Good to see you, Cuz! Or should I say, 'it does my heart good to see you, my brother'? Whooooo-weee! Yeah! Where ya going? Whatcha doin' out here, walkin' and all?"

"Good to see you too, Martin."

"No-No-No! I'm still Wavy, aye! But because I smoke so much weed some of the peeps call me 'Hazy,'" he added with a chuckle.

"Man! You still smoke that?" asked Neempau. "Better leave that stuff alone, man. It sautés the brain. Anyway, I remember when we were kids, you were always called 'Crazy Wavy.'

Both men erupted into laughter, and then Neempau continued, "I'm headin' over to Keenah's house."

"Oh, man. Jump in! Let me give you a ride, Cuz. We got a lot of catchin' up to do!"

"Sure. Thanks."

Neempau was about to toss his backpack in the backseat when he did a double take. He set it down gently and then buckled in.

Wavy shifted into gear, turned Jerry Alfred & the Medicine Beat all the way up, and peeled out.

Wavy resumed the conversation except now he was yelling over the music, "How do you like my new car? I got it about five months ago. Check out the big boss stereo system! Did you see the 20-inch aluminum rims and—?"

'Yes, yes, it's nice!" Neempau responded loudly, his annoyance evident in his voice. "What are you doing for work these days?"

"Me? I'm a valet at the Moon Lake Resort and Casino!"

"What?"

"I said I'm a valet at the—" Neempau turned the radio down, "— Moon Lake Resort and Casino!"

"Oh, nice," said Neempau.

In a tone of excitement, Wavy said, "Yeah, Yeah! I do pretty good on tips—and with the ladies. Hey-Hey! But haven't you heard? I'm going to be a big time actor someday! You think I'm gonna deprive the world of seeing this beautiful Indian face? Matter of fact, dig this, Cuz: A couple of months ago at work, the legendary director-producer Chris Eyre drove up to my valet spot! I said to myself, 'I know this is my big shot.' When I went to his car door I knew I needed to make a big impression, and I didn't wanna go all Indian on him right away - you gotta diversify, you know, Cuz? So I did my best Val Kilmer as Doc Holliday in Tombstone. So, as he got up and handed me his keys, I stood tall, gave him a Hollywood side view, and said 'Mr. Eyre, you're a daisy if you do, and I'm your huckleberry!' Then I handed him my contact info."

Neempau pretended to adjust the dial on the radio while trying to maintain a serious demeanor and asked, "Well? How did it go?"

Wavy enthusiastically replied, "Ah, Cuz. You know what? He knew I was too good to be parking cars. He just smiled at me, took his keys back, and gave them to another valet. But, you know what, Cuz? I'm working on some other huge things, too, like this business I'm gonna start up. Let me ask you, Cuz: What is the most important thing Indians all over the world need?"

Neempau swiftly replied, "Huh? Better health care, housing, education, the United States honoring all the old treaties, getting rid of stupid Thanksgiving, and—"

"Yeah, yeah, sure Cuz," said Wavy, cutting him off. "I hear. I hear ya! But something else they need. Just as important."

Neempau glanced over at Wavy, giving him a puzzled look.

"Duct tape, man!" said Wavy, revealing his business idea. "No Indian home can be without it! You can't go to pow-wow and not have some with your regalia. I'm gonna make it in all the different Tribal designs to match the regalia. I'm gonna be rich, Cuz!"

Neempau replied with a gentle smile on his face, "Umm, yeah. Sounds great, Wavy. What's with all those fireworks in your back seat? And you said you're 'good with the ladies?' Where is Naomi and your two boys, man?"

Wavy's jovial mood ceased at the inquiry. His face turned cold as he adjusted his sunglasses. He turned the radio back up and focused on the road. He accelerated the Mustang but then tersely pulled over, brought the music back down, and turned the engine off. He removed his sunglasses, revealing his moist eyes that looked at Neempau.

"She left me, Cuz," said Wavy.

He then turned forward, no longer wanting eye contact with Neempau, as he continued to explain what happened.

"It was two years ago, on the Fourth of July. I was in the backyard with the boys, getting ready to set off some fireworks, and she called me inside. She told me she didn't love me anymore, Neempau. That I was too much of a dreamer and not a doer. She wanted to know why I didn't follow the path of my dad. She said she wanted more out of life, but then she had the nerve to say that she still cares about me but I need to grow up. The next day, she left with the boys."

Wavy turned and sadly looked in the back seat and said, "I get a little depressed sometimes, so I light these fireworks. They remind me of the last fun day I had with my family. I go up to the highest mountain on the Rez and set them off, and hope my boys can see them. Like some modern, colorful, smoke signals. Aye, Cuz?" he added, with a forced smile.

Neempau quietly exhaled and said, "Damn, Wavy, I had no idea, I . . . ."

Like an actor jumping into character, Wavy put his shades back on, returned to his upbeat self, and said, "Hey-hey, Cuz, come on! Enough about me; you just got here. You gotta tell me what's going on with you. Are you finally back for good?"

Wavy restarted the engine and drove off as Neempau replied, "Well, I wouldn't say I'm back for good, but—"

Neempau paused for a moment as he floated into thought. "It's been too long since I've been back on Nipmuc land," he said. "Been thinkin' about my parents lately and what they stood for. It's time I deal with some things and this whole Thanksgiving crap. I'm sick of it. People don't get it. It's all lies— White man lies. And each year, they have this stupid so-called 'holiday.'"

"And traffic is just crazy this time of year," said Wavy.

"To me, Wavy, it's like, replaying the scene of the crime over and over. And they forget, and never mention Every Day is Thanksgiving to us. Also, we always did a Harvest Moon Ceremony around this time of year. This is not something that started with the Mayflower. Now every year we gotta see these stupid Pilgrim and Indian signs. As if that's all we're about."

As he drove, Wavy restlessly surveyed the road and said, "Yeah Cuz, crazy, crazy."

"They know nothing about us, nor do they care," Neempau went on to say, "We're just part of some fairytale dinner in 1621. Then that's the last time people hear about Natives until Geronimo."

"Geronimo!" Wavy said gleefully, "Wes Studi rocked in that movie! Came out in 1993 with—"

"That's nice, Wavy. But most people don't even realize that there are still Natives in New England. But yet the whole country cooks turkeys and stuffs their greedy faces and talk about how much Thanksgiving is an American tradition. Even my sister bought into it. I need to talk to her and get her to see the truth."

With a solemn look and a nod, Wavy said, "I hear ya. I hear ya, Cuz. Well, your Sis ain't the only one, cousin: The Rez is split on it. They even have bilingual signs up. Some say 'Enjoy the Harvest Moon Ceremony' and others, 'Happy Thanksgiving.' But I'm with ya! Whatever you need, I'm there, Cuz. But, just one thing - don't ask me to help you with Keenah. She still can't stand me."

"Geez! You two still going at it?" asked Neempau with a chuckle. "I guess some things never change around here."

Wavy snickered and said, "Yeah, well, - you know how it is around here, Cuz. People always want you to change into what they want you to be. Just like Naomi. And my dad."

"Yeah, yeah, Wavy. How is our Tribal Medicine Man?"

"Hah, you know my Pops. He's out there communing with the spirit world, universe, and all that stuff."

"You mean the 'stuff' he wanted you to do, Wavy? Don't take it so lightly. If it wasn't for your dad giving my dad and mom spiritual healing during all those difficult and crazy years, I don't know if they could've made it through."

"Of course he was there for them, Cuz! My dad is your mom's brother, after all."

"Your dad is a good man, Wavy. He's done so much for all our people. I can't wait to see him and discuss this whole Thanksgiving thing."

Wavy smirked and said, "Anyways, Cuz - he's doing a Healing Ceremony for a family up North, but he'll be back soon. There's gonna be a four-day Spirit Fire and then a Sweat Lodge Ceremony the night before Thanksgiving— I mean, Harvest Moon Ceremony. He'll be back to lead that."

"That's good, and I have an idea about how you can help me get this rolling, Wavy."

"Whatever you need, Cuz."

Neempau nodded his head with appreciation and the two men took an interlude from their dialogue as they both drifted into their own thoughts.

The Mustang reached Keenah's home. Neempau took a deep breath as they pulled into her neatly paved driveway. She had a lovely powder-yellow, modern, but modest colonial home, with a two-car garage attached to it. The yard was about an acre and well-groomed save for a few scattered maple and oak leaves resting on the Fall tawny lawn. There were black antique lamps at the edge of the red brick path, leading from the driveway to the front door. Ruby spice shrubs had grown alongside the white porch.

Wavy slapped Neempau on the leg and said, "Well, Cuz! It's been good seein' ya. I gotta get goin.' Give Keenah, George, and the kids a big 'Hey' for me!"

Neempau turned his head and did a forceful dry spit and said, "George, Huh? Oh, you mean the White guy she married?"

Wavy nervously laughed and said, "Ah, come on, Cuz! He's just as Indian as we are."

"Yeah, that's right. He has a Tribal ID," Neempau replied sarcastically. "Ah, whatever. Thanks for the lift, Wavy. I'll be seein' ya soon."

Neempau snatched his backpack out of the backseat and exited the car. He closed the door and began to stride up the red brick walkway, but spun back. He walked to Wavy's car window and tapped on it.

As Wavy rolled down the window, Neempau asked with a concerned tone, "Uh, Wavy? Why didn't you ever take the training to be a Medicine Man, like your dad?"

Wavy paused for a moment, looked up at Neempau in a solemn manner, and said, "I can't do that— I like White women and pigs' feet too much."

Neempau recoiled. "Huh?"

Wavy grinned and removed his sunglasses. "Malcolm X, 1992? You know? A Spike Lee Joint?" Wavy cut loose a hearty laugh as he reared out the driveway. Neempau shook his head, chuckled, and strolled back up the walkway.

Chapter 3

Nish

Neempau made a reluctant tap on the burgundy oak door. Swiftly, his sister, Keenah, appeared on the other side. Keenah was a petite woman with black, shoulder length, slightly curved hair. Her dark, sharp eyes were deep set and she had rounded cheeks. Her lips were small, but full, which highlighted her cupid's bow.

"Oh my gosh! You're here!" she cried as she pulled him in for a giant hug. "How did you get here? You were supposed to call me from the bus station to pick you up!"

Neempau smiled at her, looked around her home, and hesitated.

"That's ok," he replied in a low tone. "I thought I would just walk, but, uh, I ran into Wavy—"

"What? That fool? You got in the car with him? Well, I'm just glad you're here."

Keenah took a step back to get a good view of her brother and said, "Oh, Neempau. Have you been eating well? You look a little thin. Wow! Getting them gray hairs, aye, Big Bro?"

Neempau smiled as he dipped his head. Keenah hugged him again and said, "So, so good to see you!"

"You too!" said Neempau. "Where's the rest of the gang?"

"Robert and Silvia are out with friends and George is at work.

"Nice, nice," said Neempau. "Well, I know we have a lot of catching up to do. So, since nobody's here, I'd just like to talk to you about some things."

Keenah nodded her head. "Alright. Sure. Let's go to the kitchen. You hungry? You gotta be hungry; those long bus rides can wear you down. I'll put some coffee on, too."

"Uh, coffee's fine, Sis."

Neempau took a seat at the dark oak farmer's table by the window facing the backyard, while Keenah put on the brew. There was a brief interlude in the conversation as the sound of bubbling coffee resonated throughout the cozy kitchen. A cold November rain was beginning to move in. Neempau awkwardly peered about, as if out of place, and then remarked, "You have a really nice place here, Sis. You done pretty good for yourself."

"Well, I didn't do it alone," she replied with a soft laugh.

Neempau started to frown but quickly hid it behind a smile and replied, "So, how are the kids?"

"Kids?" she asked with a chuckle. "They're almost grown. Silvia is in her senior year at high school and is a starting player on the girls' Lacrosse team - for the third season in a row. Wow, hard to believe sometimes how tough she is until you see her play. Plus, she gets awesome grades, too. I can't ask for much more from that girl. Oh! She has this nice friend, also. This boy from Worcester. He's a high school honor student heading to Boston University."

Neempau noticed a Lacrosse stick standing between the refrigerator and cabinet. He went to pick it up and studied it closely.

"And, before you ask, she is also a Champion Eastern Blanket Dancer. George's mom made her a beautiful buckskin dress last year. Now, Robert.. Well, we're workin' on him. He's a good boy, but struggling in school, and all he seems to wanna do is ride his bike. And George,-"

At the mention of George, Neempau put down the stick and mumbled to himself, "I didn't ask about him."

Keenah proceeded through Neempau's inaudible protest, "Yeah, George is doing really awesome at the insurance company. He's the manager, makes a great salary. And me, 12 years at the hospital and counting," she added, with a smile of triumph.

As the sweet aroma of French Vanilla coffee encircled the kitchen, an icy, Autumn rain started pattering along the window pane against the darkening sky. The sound was coupled by the soft chime of Keenah stirring a spoonful of sugar into a large cup. Keenah handed the cup of coffee to her brother.

Neempau took a quick sip and said, "Thanks, Sis. Glad the kids are doing fine. Look, uh, like I said, you have a nice place here. I'm really proud of you – being a nurse, helping the sick, raising a family – but I think it's time for you to take a more traditional approach to things."

"What do you mean, Neempau?"

"Like this holiday? You know the way we grew up, and what we were taught. I'm trying to wake people up about this day of genocide. There is no Thanksgiving like people think it is; you know this, Sis. This is a time of mourning; the mourning of the murder of millions of Indians throughout the Northern Hemisphere that started with that villain Columbus and continued with those dirty Pilgrims." Keenah raised her eyebrows as her brother went on. "They land in Plymouth, rob the graves of all the Indians who died there from the Pilgrim's nasty diseases, and on top of that, then they call it their home."

Neempau's voice grew louder as his words became more strained. "They murder and steal the land, then have a feast. They incinerate an entire village of Indians, thank their god, and have a Thanksgiving feast. Now, today they want us to forget all that. Just go and stuff turkeys, and eat like pigs, and that's supposed to fix everything they've done. Then, in the schools they want us to dress up with fake feathers and— and—"

Neempau drew his lips in tight. His face was heavy and stressed. He then slowly drew a circle with his finger along the foggy window pane.

Keenah walked over and gave her brother a hug across the shoulders from behind. She softly asked him, "How have you been sleeping? Are you still having those nightmares?"

When he didn't respond, Keenah sat back down and stirred the spoon in her coffee. "You know," she said, "You sound almost like dad. Gosh. Time flies. Seems just like yesterday we were headin' off to a protest or—huh. And there we were, these Indian kids dealing with all that. And the schools, of course, yeah, it was rough, for sure, especially all through the elementary years. One year really stands out."

Neempau appeared hot, but refilled his cup with more brew, took a big sip and said, "Yup, I'm listening."

"It was the following Monday after Thanksgiving was over. My teacher would say, 'Good morning, class. How did everyone spend their Thanksgiving in honoring the first families of our great Country?' One of the girls in my class stood up and said, 'My mom and dad took us to the parade!' Then, there was this other boy - can't remember his name, but he had freckles, and was missing his front teeth, and had a wispy voice. He told Ms. Allen, 'I went to my grandmom's house, and she made us her best bread pudding, then we made Pilgrim and Indian hats, and ate a big turkey'. Next, like a chorus or something, several kids said, 'We went to an early morning football game, came home and had a delicious turkey with gravy, stuffing, baked ham, baked beans, sweet potatoes, cranberry sauce, candied yams, and eggnog.' Then, of course, she asked me 'What did you eat Keenah?' I don't have to tell you how I was feeling."

Neempau listened acutely as she went on, as if he were back in the classroom with her.

"So, I said, in a low voice, but trying to sound brave, 'Me and my family spent the day protesting the occupation of the White man on Indian Lands; no football game, but there was a drum. We didn't eat any turkey, either - we had deer chili, smoked salmon, succotash and bannock bread. And the Pilgrims were Tricksters—they just used Indians to kill other Indians, and then killed those Indians, too.'"

Keenah held her head up with her hand as she paused to sip her coffee with the other. Then, with a soft chuckle, she continued, "Gosh, that teacher gave me a frown that could have melted steel. Ms. Allen said in that creaky, weird, voice of hers, 'Oh my word, young lady! You cannot make up history. There is nothing of the kind in the book we studied about Thanksgiving. Sorry, Keenah—your mom got it wrong.'"

Keenah opened up the fridge and set aside some fresh salmon. She continued to search, move items around. She then stood straight and said "That teacher stood right over my desk, put one hand on her hip, and the other she used to put her finger in my face, and blabbed on, "Your *mother* should be teaching *you* to be more lady-like. I tell you, missy, if you don't pay attention to learn what we teach, you will be old, lonely, and never amount to anything.' All the other kids were looking at me like I was crazy, or from Mars, or something."

Neempau cleared his throat and said, "Tell me about it; kids can be cruel."

"One boy began yelling 'little squaw, little squaw!' Then he began to tap his mouth and let loose a stupid Hollywood Indian war cry. The teacher didn't even stop him. It seemed to go on forever.

After crying all the way home, I think I realized that day I wasn't going to be what people thought I was supposed to be."

"Well, if I was there, I would have pounded them for you," said Neempau. "You know that."

"I didn't want to get you in trouble," said Keenah. "I definitely didn't want to tell mom and dad. They would have went down there and made it worse. Especially after all dad had been through. So, I put it behind me, went to college, got my nursing degree, and that's around the time I met George and—"

Neempau released a loud uncomfortable breath.

"Hey, big Bro—George, the kids and I are happy, very happy. Look, I know how you feel about him, but he's a wonderful man, father, and husband. This is my life now. Thanksgiving is a time of family to us. I don't care what others think. And I don't mind my kids sharing in the Thanksgiving story. We still know who we are."

"Thanksgiving story? Come on, Sis, that's the whole problem. This is one big fable, and we are like some lifeless background prop that's added in or taken out. Whatever makes them look good, huh? You know what I was thinkin' as I was coming here?"

"No, please tell me." She said.

"Last month, I bet all these little hill towns were packed with Whites from all over, coming to gaze at the 'beautiful fall foliage of New England.' Just for a couple of weeks out of the year, they take notice of how pretty and colorful the trees are, but for the rest of the year they never give them a second glance. Nor do they care about them."

"What does that have to do with anything? So what? People like leaves – is that a crime?"

"You're missing my point, that's us—the Indians. Nobody knows who we are. We're only in season for a couple of weeks, and then the world goes back to black and white, but they're wrong. They're wrong, I tell you. And I'm gonna prove it. Under that black and white, there will always be red. Our blood. Our land."

Keenah rubbed her hand across her face, took a breath, and said, "Neempau is this what you came home for? I don't know what you want from me. I'm a Nipmuc Indian, just like you. We all are, whether we celebrate Thanksgiving or not. I can't be a rebel like you, Neempau, or live like Mom and Dad."

Neempau shook his head, stood up, and said, "It's not about being a rebel, Keenah. This is not about me. I'm fine. Just fine. You asked how I'm sleeping. I'm sleeping great and you know what will make me sleep better? - Putting an end to Thanksgiving. This is about exposing these liars. I want you to help me."

Keenah sighed, "Help you? Neempau, this is—"

"I'll tell you what it is: Thanksgiving is one big, fat commercial and they're selling the idea that the White man has an honest and virtuous beginning on our lands. They even changed the date of this so-called holiday to get people to spend more money on Christmas shopping. Just another way for them to profit off of our blood."

"Neempau, I think you're taking this just a little too far."

"Too far? These are the things mom and dad spent their life fighting to expose. The things you and I were taught. George has never been a traditional; I don't expect him to understand, but you, Sis, what happened to you?"

Keenah gave her brother a sideways glance, "I was going to ask you the same question, Neempau."

The house entrance from the garage opened to the patter of wet feet being wiped on the mat.

"Hello, darling!" George called from the door.

"Look Neempau, we can talk about this later, okay?"

Robert chimed in, "Hey Mom, what's to eat?"

Keenah replied, "We're in the kitchen, guys!" As George walked into the kitchen, his face wore an uncomfortable look of surprise, but he was polite.

"Hey, you made it. Welcome." George uttered, tension evident in his voice.

Neempau sat back down at the table, gave George a short nod and cheap smile, and just said, "Hey."

George was wearing a dark brown business suit. He was of medium height and build with fair skin, and dark blonde, short, cropped hair. His small, black glasses framed his brown eyes that neatly fit his slim, smooth face.

Following his dad, 15-year-old Robert rambled in the kitchen. He was thin, but healthy, with long, dark, and straight hair. He was wearing a beanie cap, black skinny jeans, and a brown BMX T-shirt. Both his arms and elbows revealed small old scars and scratches from performing bike feats at the local park.

"Robert, this is Uncle Neempau, my brother, remember?" said Keenah. "You were just a baby the last time you saw him."

Neempau joyfully stood up to embrace his nephew as Robert said, "Uh, hello, Uncle. Cool braids." Robert gave him a fist bump and hug on the back, turned to the refrigerator, rummaged through, snatched a juice box and a handful of grapes, dropping some on the floor in the process. He went on to say, "Ma, did you buy the Thanksgiving turkey yet? What's for supper? I'm wicked hungry!"

"No, my dear, we didn't get the turkey yet. But when we do we'll get it nice and fresh from the farm, like always. And for supper, I think Dad is cooking tonight," she said with a motherly smile.

Robert gulped down the drink, stuffed his mouth full of grapes, and uttered in a gurgled voice, "Hey Uncle Neempau, wanna see some of my bike tricks?"

Before Neempau could respond, George said, "Maybe tomorrow Rob, it's dark and wet out."

"Yes, Robert, your uncle's gonna be here for a while, you can show him tomorrow," Keenah added.

Robert excitedly said, "Cool, you're gonna be here for a while? Then you can come with us to the high school football game. It's really cool. Everyone goes! They have it every year, the Tuesday before Thanksgiving. They used to have it on Thanksgiving Day, but too many people were out of town, they said."

There was the clamor of jovial laughter along with stomping and wiping of shoes coming from the back, as George was preparing wild rice and baked salmon. Silvia had arrived with her boyfriend. 17-year-old Silvia resembled her mom in features, except her hair was longer and light brown, which she sported in a ponytail. Silvia had a petite but athletic figure that was coupled with her bright, appealing nature. Her boyfriend, Fredrick, was a handsome 18 year-old African American who was a senior high honor student on his way to Boston University next Fall. His mother, a close friend of Keenah, was also a nurse.

Silvia lit up when she spotted her uncle in the kitchen. She grabbed him and gave him an enormous hug, as her eyes watered. Robert, however, had taken a curious notice to what his dad was preparing to cook and said in an inquisitive but sarcastic voice, "Dad, what are you doing? Hey, Dad?"

Silvia smirked at her brother then raised her voice to speak above his "Oh my god, you're finally here!" She began to speak rapidly with great enthusiasm as if trying to tell him about her entire life within a few seconds. What she emphasized the most was her Lacrosse playing and Eastern Blanket dancing. She proudly, and loudly, stated as she turned to her boyfriend, as if to give him a history lesson, "...and the game of Lacrosse was started by Native Americans, too!"

She got to the point where she told her uncle; "I was the Lead-Lady Dancer at our Tribal Pow Wow earlier this year. It was so awesome to lead the Circle on all the dances. Next year, I want to add a pink-and-white beaded dragonfly on the back of my dress."

"Awesome, awesome, this is what we need – more tradition. This is great. I'm happy to hear that. Keep honoring our Ancestors," Neempau replied.

Silvia's boyfriend timidly leaned over and whispered in her ear, "Is this the Chief?"

Robert continued to prod his father in an uncouth tone. He questioned to the point his father could no longer ignore him and uttered, "Robert, this is wild rice. When it's done we'll put fresh strawberries on top."

Silvia answered her boyfriend with a giggle, "No, no - but he should be a Chief! This is my uncle, Neempau. Fredrick, I want you to meet my Uncle Neempau. Uncle, this is Fredrick."

"Dad! Since when do we eat this? I wanted cheeseburgers!" shouted Robert.

"Nice to meet you, sir. Oh wow! Of course, I see it; you look a lot like Silvia's mom," said Fredrick, extending his hand toward Neempau.

Neempau grabbed his hand and delivered a firm handshake, along with a strong stare to match. "Are you sayin'," he said slowly, "that I look like a girl?"

Fredrick visibly tensed and cleared his throat to reply, as he wrenched his hand free from the tight grip, "No! No, sir. I was just—"

Neempau grinned and said, "Hey, Fredrick, I was kidding. I was never a good comedian, though."

As Fredrick breathed easy, Silvia and the rest of the family got in a good laugh, then Keenah added, "OK, all you comedians, we'll be eating soon. Let's set the table."

Fredrick informed the family he had to get back home and said his farewells.

"But what's not a laughing matter is that my little nephew isn't fond of our traditional foods," said Neempau. "Robert, I think if your parents made these types of dishes more often, you would like them. These are the kinds of foods me and your mom grew up on. It's good to get back to old ways of doing things."

"Right on, uncle Neempau," Silvia proclaimed with glee.

Robert interjected with, "So, Uncle Neempau, will you come to the big football game?"

Neempau smiled, "Well, that sounds like fun, but how about the four-day ceremony on the Rez coming up, the Spirit Fire and Harvest Moon? Don't you guys wanna go to the ceremony to pay your respects and honor our Ancestors?"

George answered as he stirred the rice, "My mother is preparing a big pot of venison stew for the closing feast up there."

"But are you guys going?" asked Neempau. "This is a time of mourning. Oh, and George - I think you better check the salmon. It doesn't look like you cooked it right. I've never seen it done like that before. Looks almost burnt."

"Mourning?" Robert asked curiously.

Neempau fashioned an unexpected look of disappointment at the teen, but then beamed and stated, "Yes, Robert, a time of mourning. This is really no time to celebrate. The first Pilgrims are the ones who celebrated, they celebrated the fact they stole our land and spread their diseases, which killed almost 80% of our Tribe."

"Yes, it was a real sad time in our history, son," said George.

"Sad time?" exclaimed Neempau. "That's an understatement; they say it was 'their blessed god that sent those diseases that killed us.'— more than a 'sad time.' No, my nephew, this is *their* holiday. We have our Harvest Moon Celebration, which has been done since the beginning of time. And, Harvest Moon has nothing to do with stuffing our faces like vultures and buying junk."

"Harvest Moon? Mom, Dad, have we been to that before?" asked Robert.

"No, little boy. We haven't. We just go to the powwows. That's all I can ever remember going to," said Silvia in an irritated tone.

"Well, don't worry, kids. You guys will be going with me this year," declared Neempau.

"Alright!" shouted Silvia.

George's face became tight and pink as he opened the oven to check the salmon. Keenah took notice of George and said, "Uh Neempau, why don't we just eat; we can talk about this stuff later, okay? George, how's the dinner coming along?"

Neempau went on to state, "Yeah okay, but did you kids know that Massasoit and his warriors were never really invited to that made-up feast in Plymouth in 1621? What happened was: The Pilgrims were just shooting off their muskets and Massasoit and his warriors overheard that and thought they were under attack, and came to help. Seeing that there was no danger, they stayed, caught some deer, and fed those illegal aliens."

"Wow, I didn't know that, Uncle Neempau." said Silvia.

"Keenah, where did you put the lemon pepper?" asked George.

"And to add to the phoniness of this 'holiday,' this isn't even the White man's first Thanksgiving feast. They had already done it in Virginia around 1607. The biggest point I want to make sure you kids know about is, that these feasts were all about celebrating the killing of innocent Native Americans."

"Oh, it's beside the coffee maker, dear," said Keenah.

"Thanks, my dear." said George.

Neempau looked at Keenah, and dryly glanced at George. "Like when they burned alive those Pequot men, women, and children in 1637, then had a big Thanksgiving celebration. Or the time when—"

"Neempau, I don't think the kids need to hear all this right now," said George.

"Hey, it's just the truth; don't fear the truth, George. If I were you, I would just keep my eyes on that wild rice."

George wrestled off his cooking apron and said in a sharp tone, "Um, you know what? The food is all done, so why don't you guys eat without me? I'm going to go upstairs. I just remembered I have some important work to catch up on."

While George stormed out the kitchen, Keenah slowly walked over to the window with her eyes heavy and arms folded, gazing sadly out into the soggy darkness. She turned curtly to her brother and stated in a commanding tone, "Neempau." As he looked in her direction, she paused, but then finished her thought in a more soothing manner. "Come and get supper."

A stillness of voices gave way to the clanking of plates and forks joined by the harmony of chilly rain dancing on the windows. Halfway through their meal, a sudden clap of thunder, then lightning flashed from the distance. It startled the family and there was a collective "Whoa!" and "Wow!"

Neempau said to Keenah, "Yup, remember when Mom used to say thunder in the Winter or Fall was a powerful sign?"

"Yeah. I think Mom and Dad are trying to give you a sign."

Neempau sat straight up but tilted his head a tad as Keenah proceeded to speak, "But yes, I remember. She said it was a Night of Medicine, a time when great change and healing can come."

Neempau solemnly looked down at his plate.

"Mmm, this is pretty good," declared Silvia.

"Yeah, but I still don't see why we couldn't have cheeseburgers," said Robert.

Silvia and Robert finished their food and went to their rooms. Keenah said, "Listen, Big Brother, I'm really happy to see you – it's been way too long – but you're gonna have to get along with George. You're my family, but he's my life, the father of your niece and nephew," she said, "and a Tribal member."

Neempau balked and said, "Huh, Tribal member?"

"Geez Neempau, come on. I don't know what planet you think you're on. You act as though he's the only White-looking Indian in our Tribe. Yeah sure, people like to pretend. Even other Indians like to pretend that we're supposed to look a certain way, act a certain way, to be Native. That's pure nonsense. Full-blooded this, full-blooded that. And please don't even start on Silvia's boyfriend; I don't care what race he is as long as he's a good kid and doing something with his life."

Neempau swiftly said, "Hey, hey, I'm not racist against anybody! I just know how the real world works. Come on, Sis. Things weren't always like they are now. Now, everyone you meet thinks they are Indian. What do they tell me? That their great-grandmother was a Cherokee Princess? Oh man, all I can do is laugh to myself. Where were all these 'princesses' when our folks were getting the crap beat out of them?"

"I'm sorry, Neempau. I just don't see the world the way you do!"

"Huh? The world? Don't you remember, Sis? You talked about it yourself. Our school life? But you left out the part about how we were always treated like the outsiders in our own homeland. That was our world. Sure, there were a few kids who we could call friends, but back then everybody was picking sides. The White kids didn't like us because we were too dark, and the Black kids didn't like us because we were too light. Our Nipmuc homeland covers four states and our people are scattered within those areas so we didn't get to have Nipmuc classmates and make our own side."

Neempau paced back and forth, glaring out the window while tugging on his braids.

"And I know, I know. Nipmucs can look like anybody," he said. "Our people have been dealing with the Whites since the late 1500s. They enslaved many of our people, but when it didn't work out here, they shipped many out to the Caribbean islands, then brought in African slaves to take their place. So, of course, after all that time, our Tribe would mix with both groups. But, as far as I'm concerned, the White-looking Indians always had it easy; they could just blend right in with the master." He added with bitter sarcasm.

Keenah's jaw dropped and her face cringed as she shouted, "Boy! You really think you know how it is to walk in another's moccasins, don't you? You have no idea what you're talking about! You know what your problem is, Neempau? You're living in the shadows of Mom and Dad and you need to come out! No! Actually, you think you're living in their shadows because they didn't even think like that!"

"Now wait minute, hold on – let me say something!"

"You said plenty! 'White side! Black side! Indian Side!' Is this all you can think about? I don't know where you're going with all this Thanksgiving mess, either. I'm sure most Americans don't know about all this history. All they wanna do is have their turkey, enjoy time with family, and a day off from work, and you know what? Me too! Do you think you're living in the 60s, or something?"

"60s? Heh, I wish."

"Look at you, I mean, geez, with your 'anti-oil' patch on, walking around with a chip on your shoulder, talking about the 'White man.' And what's next, an upside-down American flag? You might as well go all the way, if you're gonna go back to the hippie days."

Neempau fashioned a big smile, as if impervious to her words, and asked, "Are you finished? Because I've heard much worse before."

"Don't you ever wanna settle down and get married? Have kids, and stop bouncing from Rez to Rez and fighting the world? Matter of fact, what happened to that 'wonderful woman' you used to live with in Northern Quebec? Or, that other one who worked at the Indian Center you told me about when you called last year? Her name was Gladys, right? That one sounded pretty serious."

Neempau smirked. "It didn't work out. Besides, I have things to do; I can't just sit back with all this crap going on."

He then mumbled, "With all these corrupt laws and courts." Then he spoke up more boldly, "The White world needs to know the truth. You said it yourself, they don't know the history and I think that's the whole problem. They go all around the world flaunting how great this Country is while the First Nations people get treated like dirt." Neempau took a big gulp of coffee and said, "Then they judge other countries and tell them how barbaric they are, while at the same time, they continue not to honor treaties and –"

"Okay! Okay, I get it. My Big Brother," she added in a slightly sorrowful tone. "I think I know why those relationships didn't 'work out,' as you put it; you're too harsh on the world, and you're stuck somewhere in that head of yours you shouldn't be."

Neempau scowled.

"Now don't give me that look. You always did that when we got into fights as kids," said Keenah. "What I'm saying is that for a woman to be with you, she's gonna have to be perfect. You don't seem to have room for anybody making mistakes. You even jumped on George over the salmon."

Neempau replied, "'Perfect?' 'Mistakes?' Believe me, Sis; I know far too well what it is to make a mistake. And I wasn't 'jumping' on George, he just didn't know what he was doing."

Keenah shook her head and said, "Well, speaking of George, and since you say you have things to do, you and him are gonna buddy-up tomorrow."

Neempau gasped, "What? I didn't come here for–"

Keenah sharply declared, "Whoa, Whoa! Slow down there, Chief. Remember, the Nipmuc way? The woman has the last say," she said with a crafty grin, "and I intend to use it."

Neempau folded his arms and looked at the ceiling.

Keenah proceeded to say, "I know you're gonna want to visit the Rez tomorrow to see some relatives, and George will be very happy to go with you."

"Sis, I'm busy, I got things to do—"

"And spending time with George is one of them. He's a good man, and you're a good brother, and you need to finally get to know one another."

She then gave her brother a kiss on the forehead and said, "Okay, it's getting late; let me take you to the guest bedroom."

47

"Whoa, guest bedroom – very nice, Sis."

"Oh, I guess you've been living off the land traditional-style?" Keenah asked.

"Huh, that's one way to put it, but it was a nice little place out in the bush. But when I was living in Northern Québec, that Reserve was only accessible by float plane. Most of the houses were small with tar-papered roofs. So this is like a palace."

"Hah- Palace? Oh, please. Just get to the room, Neempau."

As Neempau began to follow his sister, he jokingly added, "Now who's acting like our parents?"

Keenah grabbed some extra blankets from the closet and brought them to the room. While Neempau was getting settled in, he noticed an old family picture on the wall, next to the closet. He removed the picture from off the wall and gazed at it as he sat on the bed.

"Mom was beautiful, huh, Sis? And Dad, sitting there with those denim bell-bottoms on," he added with a nostalgic chuckle.

Keenah sighed. "Yup, and look in the background. You can see a tiny piece of that big blue van we had. Gosh, we went all over the place in that," she said with a smile. "It was cute, though, like a big toaster on wheels."

Neempau's eyes beamed as he recalled where the picture was taken, "Oh yeah, yeah, I remember this! This was at the Mount Wachusett Rally when Mom and Dad where protesting the cutting of the old growth forest. Hah, I remember when we went down by that little stream, and you picked those flowers and got stung by that bee. Whooolee, did you scream," he laughed. "I remember Mom saying those developers were frightened out of their pants. They thought it was some ancient warrior spirit scaring them off the land."

Keenah chuckled. "Yeah, and as I recall, you were crying, too, and didn't even get stung."

Neempau laughed. "Yeah, sure. I was crying because—" Suddenly, the laughter stopped and his face descended. He cleared his throat as he put the picture back on the wall. "I was crying because—I don't remember why. Uh, it's been a long day, I'm gonna get to sleep. Goodnight, Sis."

Chapter 4

Yau

Following a not so restful night, the next day, Neempau was awakened by his niece and nephew who were standing over his bed. "Good mornin', Uncle!" they shouted.

Robert said, "Come on, Uncle Neempau, come outside! I wanna show you what I can do on my bike!"

While Neempau rubbed his eyes, he replied in a groggy voice, "Uh, sure, OK."

Keenah walked to the door and announced, "Good morning! I'm preparing a big breakfast for everyone. Come on, you two; let your uncle get dressed."

Shortly thereafter, Neempau was sitting on the front porch on that crisp fall day, waiting for breakfast, while watching his nephew on his bike.

"That was a Bar Spin! Next I'm gonna do a 360," yelled Robert.

He sped fearlessly towards a makeshift ramp. As Robert sailed over the top, he jerked up the front end of the bike. Simultaneously, he pulled up his knees and twisted the back end of the bike completely around.

"Nice! Whoa, be careful kid!" shouted Neempau.

Silvia came out on the steps to join her uncle and said, "Man, that was some rain last night. But it looks like a new world today with the Sun out."

"Yeah it was. That's what I love about Nipmuc land the most, you never know what kinda weather you're gonna get," Neempau replied.

Silvia's mood took a solemn turn as she pulled in her lips and said, "Mom never talks about Grandma and Grandpa, too much. Can you tell me what it was like growing up with them?"

Neempau looked at her seriously for a moment, then smiled tenderly. "They were the best. They weren't afraid of anyone and cared deeply for Indian people everywhere. I remember–I must have been around nine or 10...." he said, trailing off. "Hold on Silvia, let me get your brother over here; I want him to hear this too. Hey Robert! Pedal on over here, will ya?"

"Okay, Uncle Neempau, but watch this Tailwhip first!"

Once the boy completed his bike stunt, he pulled up to the porch.

"Wow, kid! Don't hurt yourself on that bike," said Neempau. "I was telling your sister about your grandparents and I want you to hear this, too. This happened back when I was a little younger than you, Robert. We were invited to partake in a parade in Plymouth, Massachusetts. There were a lot of tensions and protests around that time; people getting beat up, arrested, and the so-called Plymouth Rock being attacked. The town officials were trying to put a positive spin on everything to ensure they wouldn't lose tourism, so they invited members from each of the local Tribes to participate in the parade. Also, several Tribal people from Upstate New York and Quebec showed up, too."

"Mohawks are from New York, right?" asked Robert. "There are a lot of Tribes in Québec, right?"

"Yeah, so anyways, they put us up in this fancy hotel. I remember me and your mom scouting through the hotel, playing with the ice machines, then bangin' on people's doors and running away. When we got back to the room, it was full of people and they were singing on the Water Drum. There was this huge abalone shell burning Sweet Grass and Sage. It sure made the room smell good, plus it covered up the smell of all those cigarettes going. I'm surprised the smoke alarm didn't go off." Robert and Silvia laughed. "Well, the next day came and we all went down to the parade grounds. They gave all the Indians front row benches, in a VIP section, along with town officials and other dignitaries. I was sitting about five feet away from the announcer at the podium who was dressed in a Colonial outfit—"

"Did he talk with a funny accent, like, from London or something?" Robert asked.

Neempau chuckled. "Yes, he had a British accent and was loud. He grabbed the mic and said,

'Okay, ladies and gents, let's please rise as we open up our festivities by singing The Star Spangled Banner!' Everybody at that moment began to rise, except the Indians. I remember the guy in the brown suit near my father – I think he was the Mayor – giving all of us an angry look. Then I noticed everyone was staring at us, as if in shock. Man, oh man. There were about 50 Indians on those benches and every one of them sat through the entire Star Spangled Banner. Heh, they all loved your grandfather."

Neempau began to excitedly move his hands as he spoke, as if leading an orchestra.

"As soon as the song was over, my dad went over to the podium and said to the announcer, 'Excuse me, but I need to use this.' The announcer, who I think was in a bit of shock, or maybe he thought this was part of the opening someone forget to tell him about, stepped aside as my pops took the microphone. My dad looked behind him in the direction of all those dignitaries sitting to the right of us. Next, he turned back around, looked out across to all the spectators who were holding colorful balloons, streamers, wearing Thanksgiving hats and other Thanksgiving garb, and said, 'Pardon me, ladies and gentlemen, but I come before you with an urgent message about the truth of Thanksgiving. Before you carve that turkey or slice that pumpkin pie, please consider the fact that the true feast of your spoils is off the blood of our Ancestors, and your table is set on top of their desecrated graves. Ladies and gentlemen, we as the original people of this land have not come here to ruin your celebration, but to tell you; your carnival is our memorial, and your parade is our death song. We only seek justice for the genocide and–"

George opened the door and cut off Neempau's story. "Okay, folks! Come on in for some good ol' breakfast!"

Silvia and Robert cut loose a simultaneous, "Aaah, man. Wait, Dad!" Robert added, "Wow! That's a cool story, Uncle. Then what happened?"

Neempau stood up, glanced sharply at George, then looked to the kids and said, "Aah, well, not too much more to tell. Next thing I remember, the cops were escorting us out. It's getting cold out. Let's go in and eat."

After the family ate their big spread of scrambled eggs, hash, toast and milk, Neempau headed off to the bathroom to clean up for the day's trip. George was also getting ready in his bedroom when his wife walked in and said, "You know why I love you so much?"

George gave her a half smile while he was putting on his sweater and replied, "Is it because I put up with your pain-in-the-butt brother?"

Keenah laughed as she came in for a hug, and then helped him straighten out his sweater. "Well, that's part of it," she stated with a chuckle. "But really, because you're the best father and husband in the world – no Nipmuc gal could ever do better."

"Can I ask you something?" George said in a serious tone."

"Of course, dear."

"Do you think your dad would have loved me?"

"Yes, I know he would have, what's not to love? Listen, darling, Neempau is just going through some changes. Don't let his behavior upset you. And once he gets to know you, he's going to love you, too."

"Well, I wouldn't count on that."

"Don't worry George," she chuckled, "I know you and my brother are gonna have a great time today."

George raised his eyebrows and said, "Ah, I sure hope so."

Shortly afterward, Neempau, having finished cleaning up, made a few phone calls, and was now sitting in the living room watching the weather report, as he waited for George.

"It's a beautiful, sunny Fall day outside the WNDN Channel 18 studio! Today's highs will be in the low 50s, tonight dipping down to about 40 degrees. Perfect weather all week as we approach Thanksgiving Day! We'll be right back with more weather after this word from Snoods!"

A short, rotund, White man is his late 50s appeared on the screen. He had soft eyes, a friendly face and was sporting a medium size beard. He was wearing a brown modern suit, but also had on a Colonial style Pilgrim hat. The hat was extra large, even for that style. Instead of the traditional square buckle in the middle, there was an emblem of a turkey.

"Huzza –Huzza-Huzza! Hello there, all Ye Pilgrims! This is Mondo Snood of Snood's Farm Famous Turkeys! Bring the whole flock down to Snoods to get the biggest and tastiest farm-raised turkeys! And remember, our farm is small, but our Snoods are huge. So–"

With a sudden click, Neempau turned off the television. He leaned over to glance out the window in the direction of the driveway as Keenah walked in.

"Okay, Big Bro! George will be right down. I'll go warm up his car and–"

"Uh, Sis, that won't be necessary."

Just as she asked what he meant, there was a car honking its horn in her driveway. It was Wavy. Keenah donned a sullen look at Neempau, "Are you kidding me? What is he doing here?"

"Me and Wavy have some serious business to take care of," said Neempau. "I wish you were coming, but if Georgey-boy wants to tag along, well, whatever, I guess. But I want Wavy to drive."

Keenah shook her head while cutting her eyes at him, "Business. Uugh. Riding with that pothead idiot? He doesn't do anything but play with fireworks, thinks he's living in a movie, and gets high all day. He's like an overgrown teenager. No wonder Naomi left him."

"Aw! Come on Keenah, cut him some slack. To me, it sounds like Wavy's trying. He is working down at the casino, you know."

Keenah balked. "Works? You mean when he shows up. I know all about his valet job down at Moon Lake. He's always late or doesn't show up, at all. He harasses the famous patrons, and I heard he's got four complaints already. Everybody's laughing at him, Neempau. He would have been fired a long time ago if people didn't have so much admiration and respect for his father. It's like, nobody wants to be on the outs with the Nipmuc Medicine Man."

"Ooh, Sis, take it easy, will ya? Besides, Wavy thinks your husband is a great guy."

Keenah folded her arms and sharply said, "Fine, fine, but I don't want him getting you and George in any trouble."

Upstairs in his bedroom, George gazed into the mirror, exhaled deeply, then trotted downstairs. George put on his best smile and said to Neempau, "Well, guess we're off to the Rez. Haven't been there in a while myself; it will be nice to see some family."

Neempau smirked, "Yeah, let's go; Wavy's waitin' outside."

As the two men headed outside, the gregarious Wavy jumped out of the car and charged over to greet them. He jumped up and, in between George and Neempau, grabbed on each of their shoulders as if using them for a balancing beam and started kicking his legs in the air while shouting, "Yes, yes and yes! This is what I'm talkin' about! I got my cousin and my other cousin!"

As George and Neempau separated to go to the car, Wavy almost fell on his face but managed to catch himself with his hands, but not before a fat marijuana joint dropped to the ground. Wavy looked up from the edge of the driveway, he saw the curtain pulled back as Keenah stared at him with disdain. Wavy picked up his joint and offered Keenah a salute just as she hastily shut the blind.

George was getting in the back seat of the Mustang and Neempau was standing there with his arms folded peering at him. George glimpsed back at him and said, "Well, what? Get in the car."

Neempau retorted, "Did you think we're gonna be chauffeuring you around the Rez?"

George took a deep breath as he got up and said, "Fine, no problem. I'll sit in the front."

While George made his way to the front seat, Neempau mumbled under his breath, "Yeah, actually I know you'd love to see me taking a back seat."

"Hey man, you know what? Why don't I just take my own car and follow you guys?" asked George angrily. "Or better yet, let's just forget the whole thing!"

Wavy stepped in and shouted, "Whoa, whoa, cousins, First Nations folks, come on! Let's have peace in the Northeast!"

Neempau grudgingly said, "Okay, okay, yeah. George, just sit in the back. Whatever, Mr. Insurance Man. Hey Wavy, he's an insurance guy – kinda like a Bureau of Indian Affairs worker, right? They take all your money, give you back a tiny little bit, then pretend they're doing you a favor."

Despite the ridicule, George simply shook his head as he moved to the back seat. Finally, the three men were all in the car.

"Okay, Wavy, did you get what I asked for?"

"I sure did; check-them-out, Cuz."

Wavy had made and printed out petition forms. They stated, 'End Thanksgiving! Let us not celebrate the loss of millions of Native Americans'.

"This is good – real good, Wavy. We are gonna hand these out all over the Rez. I bet we can get over 1000 signatures today alone. Once we get all these papers filled, we'll send it off to the State."

Wavy cranked up the radio and sped down the road as George shouted, "Hey Wavy, what's with all these fireworks?"

Chapter 5

Napanna

"This is a nice car, Wavy, love the interior. One of my staff had this same model Mustang."

"That's sweet, Cuz. What color is his?"

"It was silver."

"Nice, tell me where he lives; maybe we can race sometime."

"Well, sad to say that he had to get rid of it. He started having these really bad panic attacks or something. Got to the point where he couldn't drive. Poor guy has to take the bus to work now."

Neempau tensed his eyebrows and slightly tilted his head down toward his left shoulder. In a matter-of-fact tone, he asked, "What do you mean, George? What's that all about?"

"I don't know, he was hospitalized and—"

A sudden jolt and buck caused the fireworks to bounce off the floor. The car began to shudder. Wavy managed to hobble the Mustang over to the side of the road along the main highway. The men got out to see what the trouble was. It was a flat in the right-rear tire.

There was a collective moan and groan, as Wavy shouted, "Have no fear, Cousins! As you can see, this Stallion is brand spankin' new. Everything fully insured and under warranty. I'll call the company and they'll send someone right out to fix this Pony. We won't have to lift a finger."

George and Neempau examined the damage. Wavy got back in the car and called the insurance company. Between the cacophony of passing cars, buses, and tractor-trailers, Neempau shouted, "We should just fix this. It's a simple flat!"

George replied, "Well, he is calling his insurance. That's what they're paid to do, so—"

Neempau gave a sigh of irritation and said, "Whatever, we will just sit on this road all day waiting for a tow truck to do something that we can do in ten minutes." He folded his arms, leaned on the trunk and glared at the passing traffic.

George paced around the car, then looked down, kicked some gravel and laughed to himself while shaking his head. As he glanced in the car, he noticed Wavy looked distressed and appeared to be arguing on the phone.

Wavy got out of the car as he wiped his forehead. He donned his best smile and said, "Hey! You know what, cousins? The insurance company is too tied up today. They apologized over and over and are sending me four brand new tires. So, what the heck, we can fix this ourselves."

They got the car jacked up and were putting on the spare as another car pulled up behind them.

A middle-aged man eagerly jumped out of his car and rushed over to them and asked, "Oh, rats, do you gentlemen need any help, or anything?"

George replied, "Thanks, but I don't think so."

The man briskly replied, "Are you sure? You need a phone? Anything?"

Before any of them could respond, the man said, "Say, uh, you guys are Native Americans, right?"

"Yup!" said Wavy as he tightened the bolts of the tire.

The man's face lit up and he said, "Ah! I knew it. I knew it. Um, I just love your casino. And the buffet is superb! Do you think you guys could–"

"We're Nipmuc Indians," said George. "Our Tribe doesn't own a casino."

The man's smile faded and was replaced by a look of confusion. Wavy had stood up, cleaning his hands off on a rag, and said to the man, "Now about that help, do you have any spare–"

The man cut in and said, "Uh-uh-um, you know what? I just remembered—I'm late for a doctor's appointment."

Neempau said, "Wait a minute, what do you think about Thanksgiving and what it did to Native people? I have this petition here–"

"Yes-yes, those are nice," said the man, forcing a polite smile. "I'll mail out a donation to that— uh Indian College fund, or that other thing there."

In the blink of an eye, the man was in his car and pulling back onto the highway. Just as he sped off, Wavy yelled, "Hey! I work at the casino, does that count?" he laughed. "Come on down and I'll park your car!"

Wavy and George laughed as Neempau cut his eyes at the departing vehicle and said, "Typical."

George said "Oh yeah, Neempau, you were asking about my staff member?"

"No, forget it; it's nothing. Let's go."

The Mustang was back on the road and good as new as they approached the Nipmuc homeland.

Up ahead there was a large marker that read, 'Welcome to Nipmuc Land, Established Circa 30,000 BC.' It was a nostalgic trip back to the Reservation for Neempau as he made somber glances at roads he'd walked as a boy and lakes he fished with his father, Wavy, and several other Nipmucs.

Concurrently, George was preoccupied reading all the various labels on the fireworks scattered about the back seat floor. In a voice of excitement, Neempau said, "Hey, there's Cedar Road! At the end of it is a wooded path that leads to the train trestle over the river. We used to walk down under the trestle and fish for shad. Remember that, Wavy?"

Wavy was rubbing his marijuana joint back and forth, over his nose, as he responded, "Uh, well, kinda, Cuz. Anyway, that train doesn't cross there anymore, the bridge is too weak. Hey, you're a rodbuster. Call up some of those crazy Indians, you been living with up North, to come fix it."

Neempau smirked and said, "Huh. I'm not an ironworker anymore."

"Geez, when was the last time you were here, Cuz?" Wavy asked.

Neempau took a deep sigh and said, "A little over ten years ago when my mom passed. Soon as the funeral and Crossing-over Ceremony was done, I was outt'a here." Neempau paused to clear his throat. "But yeah, yeah, I do remember that bridge shaking like crazy when the train went by."

George added, "Yeah. It's too bad, they should have repaired it; it's such a historic bridge."

Neempau sneered at George and asked, "What do you know? You grew up in the city."

George replied in a quiet voice, "This is where my mother was born. She grew up here. My parents moved to the city because that's where the jobs were. Some people had to leave, Neempau. After all, you haven't been here in a long time."

Neempau whipped his body around to the back seat, gave George a cold look, and chided, "Hey! What I do is my business. Where I've been and why is none of yours. It's because of Nipmucs, like you, celebrating this BS Thanksgiving – that's what's ruining our traditions."

George's face soured, and he was about to reply.

Wavy jumped in and said, "Cousins, cousins! Please! Come on; let's have a good time. Neempau, we're gonna stop by the Ceremonial grounds later. They're setting up for the Harvest Moon Ceremony."

Neempau shouted, "Good! Finally get to be around others who really know what this time of year is about."

George sneered, shook his head. He made rabbits ears with his fingers behind Neempau's head.

Wavy caught the action out of the corner of his eye and grinned.

"Hey, hey, uh, Cuz?" Wavy inquired to Neempau.

"What?"

"Well, I'm just wondering, Cuz," he said, with a smile, "since you've been away so long, can you still say it?"

Neempau smiled and then turned to Wavy, "Of course, I can still say it."

Wavy laughed, "Well, I'm listening, Cuz."

"Lake Chargoggagoggmanchauggagoggchaubunagungamaugg."

"Whooo-wee! Damn! You still got it, Cuz!" shouted Wavy.

They spotted four Nipmuc males, in their late teens, walking toward the park. Two of the guys were wearing extra large jackets with the hoods pulled over their head: one black, the other green. Another teen was wearing a black leather coat and winter hat with a Nipmuc Medicine Wheel embroidered on it. Another was wearing sunglasses and had on a backwards baseball cap with the letter 'B' on it. "Hey, over there." Neempau declared. "Let's get them to sign and take these petitions."

"Are you sure?" asked Wavy.

"Yes, it's okay, pull over." Neempau replied.

As the car slowed alongside them, Neempau said, "Hey there, young warriors."

The youth with the 'B' cap said, "Yo, what do you guys want?"

"I have this petition here to end Thanksgiving. We're gonna get rid of this holiday."

The teen in the green hoodie suspiciously glanced in the car and said "Yo -dog, are you guys trippin' or what, son?" He turned to his friends and laughed.

Neempau got out of the car. The four of them took a few steps back. They all had good height but Neempau was taller.

He held out the petition and said "I'm not 'trippin, son.' I'm doing this for you guys. This is about letting the world know Thanksgiving should not be celebrated."

The teens gave each other a puzzled glance.

George looked at his watch and pressed his lips together as he observed from the rear window.

The teen in the 'B' cap said, "Thank you, sir, I feel you. You see, Wayne, this is what I've been sayin' – we need leaders to speak up."

Wayne was wearing the winter Tribal cap. "I know," he replied. "Hey Wavy, nice ride. You got that?"

"I told you before, Wayne, I got nothing for you," Wavy stated.

George and Neempau gave Wavy a sharp glance.

The young man with the black hoodie had cupped his hands over his mouth to warm them. He then gave Wayne a little shove and said, "For real Wayne, you're not smoking around us anyway."

"Take this and sign it. See if you can get this whole page filled," Neempau said.

"Ok, for sure, sir," replied the youth with the 'B' cap.

"And you," said Neempau, "Wayne, is it? Don't smoke that poison. How do think they stole all the land?" Neempau glanced at Wavy, "They kept our mind in a fog with booze and drugs."

As they pulled away, the dual exhaust created a thick, white puff as it hit the cold air.

Once the car was out of sight, the youngster with the 'B' cap closely examined the petition. He crumpled it in a tiny ball and dropped in down the sewer drain.

Their next stop on the Nipmuc Reserve was to visit old man, Chunkoo Leaper, better known as the Frogman. He was a 76-year-old Vietnam Veteran who lived just off Nippi Path. The Mustang decelerated and crawled along the dirt road, crunching against dry pine needles, acorns, and small twigs. Adjoining each side of the path were numerous elm and oak trees still holding on to a few tawny leaves beset by tall, cold, and still pines.

Neempau curiously gazed up at one of the large unadorned trees as they gradually passed it by. He observed a large flock of crows bursting up from the cold and twisted branches, like glossy black sparks shooting into the blue sky. The Frogman lived in a faded beige double-wide trailer home at the end of the lane, which also served as his place of business. There was a large makeshift sign made from plywood, nailed next to his front door, that read: 'CIGARETTES & DREAMCATCHERS 4- SALE.'

Just as they approached the home, the Frogman opened up the door. There were two squirrels lounging on his top step, but they scurried under the trailer as the old man came forth.

The Frogman's skin was light brown, wrinkled and creased around the edges of his small dark eyes. The whites of his eyes had small broken blood vessels, which made him appear permanently intoxicated. His face and neck had a few small moles including one under his sparsely filled mustache. He was missing his front teeth and appeared to be chewing on his own cheeks, at times. His long gray hair was styled in a loose ponytail. He had on his worn brown boots, black sweatpants that were pulled up above his navel, and a thick red flannel shirt tucked into the waistband of his pants. As the Frogman spied the oncoming horse, he crouched a bit, and made a visor with his thick weathered hand over his bushy eyebrows.

The men stepped out of the car and the Frogman proclaimed in his loud but raspy voice.

"Jaaaaaack Rabbit! Soak my feet in succotash! That there is a little Stoneturtle!"

The Frogman held on the handrail as he came down the steps and limped toward Neempau.

"Get on over here 'n give ol' Frogman a hug! Jaaaaaack Rabbit! I wondered what happened to you, boy! Aaah and I see you came with Marijuana Martin and, and another one I aint seen in a bit—Gray Owl," he laughed harshly, "No, No, um just teasin; jus-teasin' Come, come on in- I got some venison stew on the stove."

George and Neempau walked inside, but Wavy told them he'd be in shortly as he strode to the far side of the trailer home.

The Frogman hollered over to Wavy, "Hey there! Get away from my propane tank with that! You go on into the woods there with your dang holy-smoke!"

Just as Wavy walked away from the tank, the Frogman called out again, this time in a more thoughtful tone, "Have you heard from Naomi and the kids?"

Wavy didn't reply and headed towards a small path through the brush.

Once George and Neempau entered the small home, they noticed five shelves full of cigarette cartons, on the left, and dozens of dream catchers of various sizes, hanging from the wall, on the right. Also to the rear of the trailer, you could see his bed but it looked more like a stack of old tattered blankets. Above it was a large stuffed deer head that appeared to be in need of a good dusting.

George and Neempau settled in around the little kitchen table, which had a roll of sinew, beads, pliers and wooden hoops placed on the side. The Frogman hobbled into his chair in front of the supplies and began to work. At least five minutes went by without the Frogman looking up from his craftwork, as if he didn't know or care that he had company.

Neempau and George sat quietly as they watched the old man's worn and slightly shaking fingers weave the dream catcher's web. A few more minutes had passed; they gave each other a puzzled glance just as the Frogman forcefully shouted, "Grown men!"

The two jolted in their seats as they attempted to respond, but garbled their words.

"Grown men," said the Frogman in a milder tone, "serve themselves around here. The bowls are in that cupboard. Get some of that stew. I made it the other night."

With a sigh of relief, they rose to grab some stew as Wavy walked in, his eyes glazed and pupils small. Wavy swiftly snatched the largest bowl he could find and scooped up a hefty serving of the dish. Between the din of slurping potage, and Wavy coughing intermittently, Neempau asked the Frogman, "So, how have you been? You got a nice business going here."

The Frogman glanced up from his work and said in a harsh voice "Huh! Business? This is the only thing keeping me from killing someone." He then angrily cut his eyes at the men sideways. He plunged into a robust laugh exposing his naked gums. "Juuuus teasin', juuus teasin', we old timers sure miss your parents, Neempau. When I got back from 'Nam, the same dang day I returned, your folks was heading down to D.C. to march in a big protest for the return of Indian lands. My leg got all shot up, over there, in Vietnam; I was in too much damn pain at the time to head down there with them," he said as he rubbed his knee. "So all of us who didn't go, we lit a Sacred Fire for all who went. We knew they was gonna need some big prayers. The Feds and the police were really busting up a lot of people back then; they didn't care whether it's a woman or not."

The Frogman paused, as he held up a dreamcatcher, and squinted one eye.

"We kept that Sacred Fire lit until everybody returned safely. We sang on the Water Drum, burned Tobacco through those there nights. Some folks fasted and gave out prayer ties to every Indian they ran into, even the ones who was so drunk, they didn't know if they was comin or goin', yeeep-yeeep; they're part of us too." He added with a nod, "I know you don't recall; you were jus' a little bitty thing still crapping in your pants. And this one sittin next to ya, his wife wasn't born yet. And Martin— when everybody returned from DC, your dad held a special Sweat Lodge Cleansing Ceremony. Yeeeep."

Wavy gulped down the food and appeared indifferent when hearing the accolades of his father.

Neempau, however, beamed and said, "Wow, I wish I could remember that one. Anyways, that's why I'm here. I'm trying to pick up where they left off; and I'm starting with putting an end to this stupid Thanksgiving celebration. The White world should be ashamed of themselves, never mind celebrate. I got this petition here—"

The Frogman tilted his head toward the ceiling, scrunched his eyes and stroked his throat, "Humm—end Thanksgiving? Well, sure would make a lot of turkeys happy, wouldn't it?" He laughed and coughed a bit, "Huh— I always went to the Harvest Moon Ceremony, anyway."

He went back to weaving the dreamcatcher. "I tell ya son, I seen a lot of death and a lot of protests through my years. I just think back on how long it took us, Indians, just to have our freedom of religion. It wasn't in the 1700s with the Constitution. No. Nooo. It wasn't until 1978 that we got the freedom to worship in our traditional way," he declared with a thump on the table. "I fought for this Country. Just like a lot of our people did. We served proudly in every war. Every war the United States was ever in.— Draft? Heh! We were never worried about no draft. When our home's in trouble, we defend it. Simple as that. This is what they don't understand about us; why we still fight. We're still fighting for our home. Now take a gander at this here dreamcatcher. Nice work, in'it?"

"Excellent work, the best I've seen," said George.

"So, the plan is to put an end to Thanksgiving. Well, I know this, the White man moves very slow when it comes to Indians. Unless they are rushin' in here to get my great cigarettes prices! Well, now it's almost time for me to go to the Great Council Fire in the sky, but whatever you boys need me to do— I think I've got one more battle in me."

Neempau smiled, "Good, signing this petition will–"

There was a subtle rap at the door. The Frogman pulled himself up and shuffled over to see who it was. It was two young ladies and man.

One of the women said jovially, "Hello, sir. We would like to buy ten dreamcatchers and two cartons of smokes, please."

The Frogman put the goods in a brown paper bag. He passed her the bag but continued to hold on to it. He then said, "Remember, if you're having negative dreams, these here dream catchers will protect you from them."

"Really?" She asked

"Of course, but you have to believe. And remember: don't go to that other Tribe. I got the best prices around."

The woman smiled.

Neempau sat at the table with his arms tensely folded while he watched Wavy eat.

The female looked to the right and noticed the men sitting at the table and said, "Pardon us, but we're students at Cord University, and are currently studying the local Tribes for a class project. Can any of you spare some time to share some of your history and culture?''

The student made an uneasy chuckle. "I'm mean, like, I know you guys don't live in teepees or ride horses, anymore. But any help for this project would be–"

Her remark was interrupted by a thud when Neempau leaped from his chair. Neempau scowled and bit his bottom lip as he confronted the undergraduates.

"Project?" he shouted at them in a mocking tone. "Do we look like a class project to you? What the hell! Do you think you're at the zoo?"

The male of the group came to her aid and explained, "N-No- no, sir! It's not like – it's not like that, at all. It's Native American Awareness Month and we're here to learn about your people."

Neempau nodded his head and let loose a cynical laugh. "Native – American –Awareness –Month, are you joking? Gee, thanks, my

Tribe has maintained a culture, history and society for over 30,000 years on this very ground. And you people wanna give us a month while the White culture, which has been here for a few hundred years, gets all the other months?"

The male student replied, "But sir, we want to learn and–"

"You don't wanna learn, you wanna 'dance with wolves.' I see it everywhere I've been. You college kids come on our land, looking to be entertained for a few weeks then go back to your beer bong parties and real school work. You never want to hear or see the real issues we have here."

"But that's why we are trying to learn," the male said.

"Why don't you start by learning the real story of your upcoming 'celebration' then? Thanksgiving was nothing more than a celebration of the slaughter and removal of Indian people everywhere. Or learn how the Federal Government has robbed our Tribe at every turn. Also, how Native American youth are so hopeless and hungry that on some Reserves, they resort to sniffing gas as young as eight and nine years old."

The other lady exclaimed, "Yes, I did read about that extensively. Some of it was due to–"

"Read about? Try living it! Alcoholism, diabetes, extreme poverty. Right here in the great USA, you have old people freezing to death due to lack of funds to keep themselves warm, and you wanna carve a turkey?" he added with a sarcastic laugh, "You people have some nerve. With all your parades and car sales. What's any of that have to do with learning about the First People of this land? Not only that, but the Feds don't care about our blood or our people! They only care about the money they can make off us by making shady deals, with shady people, despite what's true, or just."

The Frogman was cutting leather into thin strips to wrap around the wooden hoops. Wavy had eaten all his stew and was munching on the Frogman's sugar-free cookies. George sat at the table with his hand over his mouth, his eyes fixed on the Frogman's hands.

The woman holding the bag of smokes and dreamcatchers whispered to her friends, "We should go."

Neempau said, "You kids are smart, right? Look at the laws of our Country. They stay the same for everybody. But Indian law in the Bureau of Indian Affairs changes all the time, depending on how much money, or depending on the Tribe. George. Wavy. Let's go, I said what I had to say."

Neempau said his farewells to the Frogman, and he hastily bustled past the students. The undergraduates departed to their vehicle in silence with somber expressions. Just before they left, Wavy walked over to them. In an upbeat mood and with a little bounce, he told them, "Hey, uh, I got a little secret to tell ya: our Tribe never lived in teepees or rode horses, but let me tell ya, if you ladies wanna interview me, I can take you over to my wigwam," he said with a seductive flair, "I'll have you know, I'm a future superstar and–"

"Wavy! Let's go!" shouted Neempau from the car.

Once Wavy made his way back to the car, Neempau enquired, "Hey, Wavy, why don't you let me drive a bit? You look a little sleepy."

Wavy shouted back, "For suuuure, Cuz!"

The Nipmucs proceeded on their way, making several stops at relatives' homes and familiar locations. They managed to get 14 people to sign the petition.

"Hey, why don't we stop by the Nipmuc Tribal Office?" said Neempau. "See what kind of support we can get there."

George and Wavy agreed. By the time they arrived at the Tribal Bureau, only one person was there. Councilperson Harriet Vickers was finishing up filings for a Nipmuc land claims case. She was an attractive 32-year-old, enthusiastic, very intelligent, and a newly-elected addition to the Tribal Council. She had recently graduated from college with her Master's degree in political science.

"Hello there, fellas. What can I help you with?" she asked in a spirited voice.

Harriet first made eye contact with Wavy, who then nervously looked to Neempau. Then she turned to George and he swiftly scratched his forehead, as if to cover his face – he also turned to Neempau.

Harriet chuckled and said to Neempau, "Um, I guess that leaves you. Are you the leader of this triumvirate?"

Neempau flinched and paused for a moment. "I- I'm not sure what that means, but we're here to talk about ending Thanksgiving, and I'm passing around this petition."

Wavy attacked the candy dish sitting at the edge of her desk. He rapidly scooped out as many chocolates as he could hold.

Harriet's serious look held a hint of a smile. She asked, "What? Are you guys joking? And look at him— he's high as a kite! Did my brother, Stewart, send you guys down here to pull a prank on me? Just because I'm new on the council doesn't mean—"

Neempau took a quick agitated breath and said, "Hey, wait a minute, this is no joke. The crime of celebrating Thanksgiving needs to end."

Wavy cut in and said, "I'm not that high – wish I was, though."

Harriet shook her head and said, "I know George, and unfortunately, Martin Jr.–"

"The name is Wavy. Call me Wavy."

"But who are you?" she asked Neempau.

"I'm Neempau Stoneturtle."

"Oh, I see – Stoneturtle." She cheerfully rose from her desk, "Your sister is Keenah; I know her. And I knew of your parents too; they did so much for our community."

Neempau replied, "Yes, thanks, that's why I'm here. Now about Thanksgiving?"

Harriet sighed, and said, "Ending Thanksgiving? I can't speak for the whole council but we have our hands full with land claims, and getting health care, and decent housing to our people. Then there's education, hunting and fishing rights; and most of all, trying to preserve our natural forests from development."

"How is the council coming along with that?" asked George.

"It's a long road, but it's worth it," she replied. "The State of Massachusetts thinks that just because they hold an illegal title to our forests, that we don't care about them anymore. Now with this whole casino craze, things are really going to get out of hand. I don't see where this Thanksgiving issue–"

"Fine." said Neempau. "I knew it."

Disappointed, Neempau grumbled and looked agitated.

"Now, wait," Harriet said. "You know, when I first heard you say 'end Thanksgiving,' it sounded pretty out there, but that's where it all started right? All these filings, claims, motions and papers, coupled with ambiguous laws and broken treaties—"

George's cell phone rang. "Excuse me," he said.

George stepped out into the lobby of the Tribal Office. He stood in front of the large bronze and oak commemoration plaque issued to the Tribe in 1996 by Governor William Weld. The plaque stated: "In Honor of All Nipmuc Veterans, From King Philip's War of 1675 to the Present." It was inscribed with a long list of names that went down the entire wall.

"Oh, hi Keenah, what are the kids up to?"

"The kids are fine, dear. I was worried about you. I just wanted to call and check to see how things are going."

George seemed to go off in a trance as he took notice of the name 'Matoonas.' He was one of George's Ancestors. Matoonas fought bravely against the English during the King Philip's War, but was eventually captured. He was taken to Boston and beheaded. Impaled, his head was placed on a pole and propped next to another decapitated Nipmuc. It was Matoonas' eldest son, who the English had executed years earlier.

"George? - George?" Keenah inquired in a tone of concern. "What's going on? How are you and Neempau getting along?"

"Huh? Me and Neempau?" he dryly replied. "Well, let me tell you-"

George paused when he heard a burst of playful laughter going back and forth between Harriet and Neempau. He could see from the hallway the two of them getting along quite well.

George made a subtle smile.

Keenah said, "Well, what happened?"

"Oh, nothing, dear, we are having a great time. A great time." he said.

"Ah! I knew I was worrying for nothing," she said, "You're all choked up, because I bet you guys are telling some 'man' jokes." She laughed.

"No, dear, nothing like that. We're at the Tribal Office."

"Oh, nice! Tell them I'm gonna bring more pamphlets on diabetes prevention."

"Sure, darling."

"Okay, I'll let you boys get back to your fun. See ya tonight, babe- love ya!"

"Love you, too, bye."

George took a breath and walked back into the office.

"So yes, the Pilgrims came looking for freedom, but since their arrival, we've been fighting for ours." Harriet proclaimed.

Neempau exuberantly replied, "Yes –yes, that's what I've been saying."

"But still, Thanksgiving has become American as apple pie," Harriet stated. "There's a lot of money and American cultural tradition involved. You know – sales, parades, football games, big family get-togethers, and so forth."

"Fourth of July!" shouted Wavy.

Harriet paused, glanced at Wavy with a perplexed look, and went on. "I'm not sure people even put a whole lot of thought into us-Natives, anymore. I have some relatives who don't celebrate it either, but they never thought to try and end it. Well, Neempau Stoneturtle, you gave me a lot to consider. I can't make any promises but I'll bring this petition to the counsel to see what they think."

Neempau gave Harriet a big smile and a nod. She returned his smile. For a brief moment their eyes met. Unexpectedly, Wavy tapped Neempau on the shoulder and said, "Alright, Cousin, now let's hit the road."

George said, "Thanks for your time. Keenah will be dropping off some health info tomorrow."

Wavy loudly said, "Okay! Bye!" He waved his left hand up high, as if to divert her attention. His right hand was busy snatching more candy.

Neempau was the last of the three to walk out of the Tribal Office. Just as he looked back in Harriet's direction, he caught a glimpse of her looking at him with a smile, but she quickly looked to her desk, upon being noticed.

Once they were back in the car, Wavy said, "Aye, Cuz! She is cute, huh?"

Neempau laughed, doing his best to ignore Wavy's inquiry.

A couple hours later, Wavy began to clear his head as they arrived at the Nipmuc Ceremonial Grounds. There were several people present making preparations for the coming Harvest Moon Ceremony and the Sweat Lodge Ceremony.

Neempau looked on, with elation, as he pulled over to the side of the road, "Yes. This is what it's all about. No stupid Thanksgiving stuff here." He peered in the backseat at George and said in a magnanimous fashion, "Come on, you might learn something."

They got out of the car and went down the trail that had two huge round stones on both sides. They shouted 'hello' to a couple of Nipmuc women who were bringing in refreshments to the helpers.

The large Sacred Circle was not far down the lane and was surrounded by beautiful and robust White Cedar trees. There were seven hand-carved wooden benches encompassing the periphery of the Round.

The inside of the circle was carefully groomed and covered with smoothed, yellowish-brown Fall grass. At it's center was a clearing for the Sacred Fire that would be lit, two days later, at sunrise for the start of the ceremony. Wavy, George, and Neempau didn't enter the Circle, for it is considered disrespectful to do so, before the ceremony.

Instead, they walked around to the side to get a look at some of the other folks who were there. Neempau presented the 'Stop Thanksgiving Petition' to everyone he saw. He was met with some resistance, a few people told him that this wasn't the place for that, while others said they would think about it.

Wavy pointed in the direction of the Nipmuc Longhouse, which sat at the edge of the woods that led to a vibrant stream. In front of the Longhouse, was a group of people singing around a big drum, and a couple of others sitting on the ground nearby. Wavy reported to Neempau, "Look over there Cuz, that's the 'Quabbin Lake Singers.' Did you hear of them? That's Spotted Crow, with his boys, and a few of his cousins."

Neempau took an attentive glance and said, "Oh yeah, Spotted Crow. The Frogman is his uncle, right? Yeah, I've heard of their drum group. They sound pretty good, too."

Wavy shook his head, "Yeah Cuz, that's the one. And it's a good thing he can sing, because that's one ugly dude. I mean, his kids are cool, but the Nipmuc Gods were not nice to him in the beauty department!" he laughed. "I run into him over at Billy Cornleaf's Breakfast Barn, all the time. He's always going on, and on, about how someday he's gonna write a book, or something."

George replied, in a serious tone, "Well, you never know."

Wavy said, "Yeah, yeah. I know. He tries."

"Plus, it would be nice for more people to know more about Nipmucs," George commented.

Wavy laughed, shook his head, and said, "Nipmucs? Nooo-body knows about us." Even the Federal Government likes to pretend we're not here. We are invisible. Hey Cuz, you can't see me!" He shouted, "I'm invisible! Heya-hey! Like the Chief! The Chief in the movie, Little Big Man!"

Wavy flapped his arms by his side, and hopped around George.

A few other Tribal members standing by at the other end of the Longhouse looked on and laughed.

Neempau smirked. He then glanced around and asked, "Where's your dad, Wavy? I can't wait to talk with him."

Wavy straightened up and replied, "Uh, he doesn't get back till the ceremonial lighting of the Sacred Fire."

At the same moment, two men appeared from another small path. Both of them were carrying wood that they placed under the arbor. They had been splitting the timber in preparation for the coming ritual. Neempau stared at the men, with a harsh look on his face, and his mouth hanging open.

As the two men walked back and forth stocking the pile, they waved to the guys. They were too far away to discern the bitter look on Neempau's face.

Neempau turned to look at George, then whipped around and growled to Wavy, "Who — who are they?"

Wavy said, "Oh, Cuz, those guys are helpers of my dad. Nice guys. I met them last year when my dad—"

"Oh, come on!" snapped Neempau. "Why are these White guys here? This is *our ceremony*. This is supposed to be *Natives only*. They don't need to be here. Don't they have their stupid Thanksgiving? They try to destroy us and then they wanna be us."

Neempau paced back and forth, in frustration, and held his head. Wavy appeared as though he wanted to console Neempau but didn't know what to say. George looked up to the sky as if he wished he were somewhere else.

"I gotta get out of here!" Neempau shouted, his voice bitter and cold. "This is all wrong. I really need to see your dad."

Wavy put his arm around Neempau's shoulder and said, "Hey, come on, Cuz, calm down. Look, let's get off the Rez. I know this great place we can go hangout and wind down. It's this bar and grill up in the city called the 'Cue & Sip.'"

Wavy went on to say, as he wiggled his eyebrows, "They have pool tables— you still love pool, don't cha Cuz? Come on! The ol'

Medicine Man will be back soon, but in the meantime, let me show you a good time. You too, George. It will be fun!"

Despite Neempau's bitter disappointment, he agreed to head up to The Cue & Sip with the fellows.

Chapter 6

Qutta

It started out as a quiet, and subdued, evening ride heading to The Cue & Sip, until Wavy began chattering about all of his girlfriends and his inevitable ascension to 'stardom and fame.' Wavy then said, "You know what, Cuz? Naomi's gonna wish she never left me. I can almost hear the phone ringing right now, 'Mr. Martin Wavy Attuck, we here at Universal Studios would be honored if you would sign on with us.' Yeah-buddy- buddy, she'll see!"

As they drove along approaching the city, George blurted out, "Hey Neempau! Look over there; that's the elementary school you and Keenah went to. Yup, that old building is still there."

Neempau's face turned sour as George's comment crudely resonated into his head like corrosive fluid, flooding and damaging his soul. He turned to the right and his eyes froze at the building of his nightmares. Without warning, his spirit was snatched from the Mustang, and thrown back into the, dark and cold, closet of his fourth-grade class:

The source of the musty dry stench that was sticking to the back of his throat, was hidden within the small gloomy abyss. To counter the blackness, the Nipmuc boy attempted to close his eyes but was forced to surrender to the flowing tears that demanded release. His weeping and seclusion went on for what seemed like an eternity, while in the classroom the holiday festivities were underway.

The children were all dressed up in paper feathers and Pilgrim hats as the First Thanksgiving play was underway. A few other teachers were preparing a grand party, with all sorts of holiday sweets, and treats for the little Thespians. The tasty delights included cookies and cupcakes made from sweet pumpkin, vanilla fudge, chocolate, and raspberry filling. There was also a plump Dutch Apple Pie and ice cream, along with small grab bags with a toy, new pencils, and a notebook.

It was now 20 minutes until school was let out for the day, and about the time Neempau was finally released from his fourth-grade dungeon. As Ms. Nelson swung the door open, Neempau's eyes squinted as the light broke through, and his nose rejoiced to the smell of the sweet goodies. He had spent close to six hours confined; no lunch or bathroom breaks. Throughout the ordeal, his natural bodily functions remained in an intense competition with time. However, the dampness in the front of his pants revealed his bladder came in second place.

The teacher towered over the boy sucking her teeth and shaking her head. Neempau asked the teacher if he could go straight home to change, but she rejected his request. She stared at him with a scowl and said, "You asked for it, now you got it! That's going to be your room for the rest of the week, but right now I want you in your regular seat. Move it! Take your seat! Your seat!"

"Your seat! Your seat, Cuz! Push your seat up. You gonna let George out of the car, or what?" Wavy said.

Neempau quickly inhaled and exhaled, wiping the sweat from his forehead, as he pulled himself out of the dark past.

They arrived at The Cue & Sip, which was located on the East side of the city. It was a medium-sized, good-looking, bar & grill and billiards hall. Wavy shouted, "Come on, cousins, let's go in! Time to have a good time!"

Neempau leaned up to let George out the car as he continued to collect himself. George took notice and asked Neempau, "Say, uh, are you alright?"

Neempau sharply replied, "Of course I'm alright. Are you alright? Come on. Let's go in."

As they walked to the door, the sound of the low thumping music was increasing with each step. Once inside the neon lit hall, the scent of sundry beer, cologne, and hot wings permeated the air. There was a mixed crowd of laborers, businessmen, and middle-aged couples enjoying the long weekend off.

George and Neempau stopped just inside the entrance, as if waiting to be seated, while Wavy swaggered over to the digital jukebox and began loading songs.

Wavy shouted, through the sparsely crowded club, to the bartender. "Hello there! Do you have Keith Secola, George Leach, or Jim Boyd in this thing?"

Neempau cautiously looked around, then nodded for George to follow him over to Wavy. With a serious tone, Neempau asked Wavy, "Are you sure about this place? How many times have you been here?"

Wavy said, "Dang! It's too bad, Cuz. Robbie Robertson should have gotten more credit for his music on the 'Color of Money' soundtrack! Oh well, I'll play the soundtrack anyway."

"Wavy!" Neempau shouted.

Wavy replied with a bubbly laugh, "Cousins, Cousins! This is my first time here. I heard some people talking about it when I was parking their car. Ain't it nice, though?" he added, while patting George on the back.

Neempau shook his head while Wavy just smiled and insisted, "Aah, come on, Cuz. Let's go play some pool. This is a great place."

Neempau cracked a smile and said, "Okay, okay, we'll play a couple games; you know I love pool."

George added, "Okay, guys, while you get the game started I'll go get some drinks. Wavy, Neempau, what would you like?"

Neempau requested a ginger ale and Wavy asked for a cold beer. Neempau gave Wavy a harsh glare and said, "Hey man. You know the ceremony starts in two days. The body is supposed to be alcohol free; it's bad enough the way you smoke that—"

Wavy cut in as he racked the pool balls. "I told you, Cuz, that stuff ain't for me. A cold beer, George, if you please."

George replied, "Well, okay, I guess Neempau or I will be driving, again. I don't drink either, Neempau."

Neempau sneered and said, "What, George? You mean you don't have your dry martinis with all your big shot 'executive colleagues' at work, or between a round of golf?"

George scoffed before proceeding to the bar. He took a seat at the long, glossy oak bar that had salt, pepper, Tabasco sauce, and a small green menu featured in front of every chair. The dish of popcorn was out of his range, resting in front of a married couple several seats down, who were sipping on White Russians.

The rustic, dark amber shelves before him were jam-packed with several dozen varieties of intoxicants in an assortment of charming, colored bottles.

While waiting to be served, he looked left of the large brass mirror, with all the liquor jugs showcased in front, and checked out the flat screen TV. He was just in time to catch the tail-end of the commercial.

"My Snoods are huge! And remember Pilgrims; you haven't seen a turkey until you've seen my Snoods! Happy, happy Thanksgiving, Pilgrims!"

George returned his attention to the bartender as she came to take his order. He got their drinks and also ordered a heap of hot wings and fries. After dropping off the drinks to the fellows at the pool table, he returned to his barstool and waited for the food. By that time, two gentlemen had walked in, and sat down in the seats next to him. They were both warehouse workers for a trucking company. The men were in their late 30s, good size, and had a hardy look. The bartender called them by name. "Hey Jasper, Chet — what can I get for you guys?" Jasper had on a black, worn down, baseball cap that fit tight on his head. Embroidered on the front in white letters was the name, 'Stoidi Freight Co.' His black hair pushed out from behind his ears and went to his shoulders. Chet was blonde with buzz cut, but bald on top. The two men ordered their drinks, but were preoccupied with Wavy and Neempau at the pool table.

Wavy was being very flamboyant as he took each shot. "Haaa-Chaaa! In your face, Cuz!" Following that, Wavy's cell phone rang, which he ignored until Neempau said, "Hey Wavy, you gonna answer it or what?"

Wavy pulled out his phone, looked at the number then turned it off and said, "Ah, it's nobody, Cuz."

The next song on the jukebox was 'Werewolves of London.' Wavy started out with a little bobbing and foot tapping. He began strutting around the pool table and let off a loud and obnoxious howling noise before he roared, "Those Twilight punks ain't got nothing on me!"

Following his declaration, he straddled the pool stick between his legs and commenced to hopping and galloping forward, while smacking the air.

Jasper and Chet were cutting their eyes at the silly scene as they slowly sipped their vodka.

Chet, in a low guttural and distasteful tone, grumbled, "Good grief. Would you look at that, Jasper? Pitiful, just pitiful. Who let the overgrown pickaninnies and smelly heathens in here?"

Jasper responded, "I know, I know, it's disgraceful what this Country has come to. Looks like mating season in the jungle over there. Must have gotten their welfare checks today. Awful. We can't go anywhere without crossing a herd of mud people. See, I told you, this is why I hate coming into the city."

George, who was sitting right next to them overheard the vitriol and was growing agitated.

Over at the pool table, Wavy and Neempau were having a ball. In a cool fashion, Wavy turned away from the table while taking his shot for the nine-ball and shouted, "Check me out, Cuz. Is this how Tom Cruise did it?"

He took the shot, missed, and sent the cue ball flying off the table and over by the ladies' bathroom. The ball rested just beneath the bathroom door. Wavy ran over to grab it while at the same time a woman was exiting the restroom. She was shaking her hands in the air as Wavy startled her with his presence. Wavy smiled and offered his hand in a shake. The woman grinned and offered her hand, but she pulled it back quickly.

"Oops, sorry!" she said. "Wet hands; they were out of paper towels."

Wavy replied, "No problem. I'm a fisherman." Then he winked at the lady, picked up the ball, and danced back to the pool table.

Chet looked on with contempt, as if he was watching a crime in progress and uttered, "Looks like the real estate around 'The Cue & Sip' is about to depreciate."

The bartender also heard the men and she said, "Hey! Look you two, I don't want that kind of talk in here. Knock it off, or leave."

Jasper responded in a look of bitterness and disbelief. "What? What? We are paying customers. What, there's no freedom of speech at The Cue & Sip?"

Following that, Jasper, who was sitting next to George, nudged him seeking affirmation and stated, "What crap huh, pal? It's always about the darkies *rights,* isn't it?"

George who was fuming and grinding his teeth shouted, "You racist scum! Those guys you're talking about are my relatives! And they're both Nipmuc Indians, as am I, you jerks!"

Jasper recoiled, gave George a hard stare, and squinted one eye, "You're gonna sit there and tell me, you're an Indian?"

"Yes, I am," said George, returning a firm stare.

Jasper took a sip of his drink, laughed, and said, "Indian, this damn fool thinks he's an Indian. Look at you. You're Whiter, than me,"

Chet joined in on the laughter and shook his head at George.

"I have nothing to prove to either of you," said George.

The married couple who had been enjoying their White Russians also observed the bigoted rant. They left their drinks, hastily grabbed their coats, and began to leave, but not before the lady had a few words for the two gentlemen.

"You know, it's racist and small-minded idiots like you that give the rest of us a bad name. Your type of behavior is so out of date. You two apes need to go climb back in your cave and stop causing trouble."

Jasper sneered at the lady and wiggled his fingers in the air and said, "Oh I see what this is: This is one big Kumbaya-fest.' Everybody is attacking us. The freakin' Cue & Sip has turned into one big 'Affirmative Action' office. Everybody is against the White man. No free speech for the White man."

Other patrons whispered to one another with a look of agitation as Jasper shouted, "Can't you see what's going on? Look at these 'people!' They get to do what they want. They run around in all them different government-supported groups. Damn Indians got their big fat casinos and free money from the Government, paid for by *my* tax dollars!" he shouted as he slapped his chest.

"And the damn colored—" he began to say, stopping himself, "— African-Americans have their NAACP, and free college, and what not! All for their little groups. What about my group? I'm a White man, so why don't I get a group and free money? I have to work for what I have! That is, when an illegal isn't stealing my job! And now I can't even have free speech? Is this America?"

"You fools are so lost, and so misinformed, that I don't even know where to begin," interjected George. "Are these the things you believe to keep yourselves locked in ignorance? Most Tribes don't have casinos, including ours. And most casinos don't make Indians 'rich' as you say. Free money? I work for a living too. Do you realize many Indians are not even recognized? Which means they get nothing, at all. Most of what the Government has taken from Indians will never be recovered."

"Yeah, yeah, sure; but you know what really gets me?" Jasper retorted, "Every time I turn on the TV, there's some minority whining about race. Why can't they drop it already?"

"Oh, so you get to decide when their suffering and grievances should be over and—"

"What's the problem," asked Neempau, with a stern look on his face. Neempau, who along with Wavy, had come over to see what all the commotion was about.

"Hey, hey, everyone! It's the holidays. Let's just settle down," the bartender said in an uneasy tone.

Jasper joked to Chet, "Yeah, that's right, it's Thanksgiving, man." Then Jasper tweaked his voice to sound like a young girl with an added twist of sarcasm and uttered, "Look at me! I feed the Pilgrims; I feed the Pilgrims!"

The two of them laughed so hard they almost fell from their barstools. Wavy, Neempau, and George bitterly looked on at the cackling duo. Then Neempau shouted, "We should have let you all starve!"

Jasper paused, sniffed, wiped his mouth, and gawked at Neempau with wide eyes, and said, "Hey, don't you know? That's your job, boy, to serve the White man."

Neempau's face was tense and hot. "Why you son of—"

Chet butted in and spoke as he turned his back to Neempau, "Hey! Tonto. Nobody was talking to you. You came over here. Now, why don't ya go crawl back up a liquor bottle, weave a basket, or some damn thing."

Neempau took a moment to absorb the comments. He released a subtle smile, reached over and grabbed Chet's drink, and said, "You know what? Instead of me crawling in a bottle, I think I'll give this drink to you."

Without a word Neempau threw the drink in the Chet's face. Chet recoiled and flailed for a moment from the stinging vodka that splashed in his eyes. His elbow knocked into another glass and it teetered to the edge of the bar. The fluid streamed down onto the floor, making a puddle of draft beer, near his feet. He attempted to get up from the stool, slipped on the beer, tried again, but before he could rise, Neempau punched him in the nose, sending him crashing over the chair. Jasper charged into Neempau, grabbing him around the waist, and slamming him to the floor. Wavy came to Neempau's aid, pouncing on top of Jasper and punching him in the ribs and face. Chet, with a bloody face, regrouped, and joined in on the action. The four men rolled and crashed around the bar, kicking, punching and knocking tables over, leaving a path of destruction. By that time, the married couple had fled The Cue & Sip, along with several other patrons.

George seemed not to know what do as he looked on in horror and dodged out of the way of flying objects. While all this was happening, the bartender had called for backup. Six large men from the back of the establishment rushed out and put a halt to the rumble. As the men were peeled off of each other, the bartender shouted, "All of you, get out, or I'm calling the police!"

Jasper aggressively pulled his arm away from the bouncer and said, "Get your hands off me," as he picked his hat up off the floor, dusted it off and put it back on.

Jasper and Chet took off first. As they went out the door, Chet shouted a threat, as he held his nose to curb the blood flow, "Better hope we don't meet again, because if we do, you mud boys are mine!"

Wavy, Neempau, and George also made a speedy departure. Since Wavy had a few too many drinks, George took over the driving. Neempau was rubbing his right shoulder and stretching his jaw as he turned to George and said, "Hey, drive a little faster."

George replied, "I can't, the speed limit it 45."

"Oh, of course, you don't want to break the rules," scoffed Neempau. "Just like you didn't want to help us fight back there. What's wrong, didn't want to upset your buddies? I don't even want to imagine what those guys were saying before me and Wavy got over there. And I bet you just sat there and took it."

George sighed. "Let's just go home."

Wavy was laying down in the backseat, holding his head and moaning. "Oh, where is my Naomi? What are my kids doing tonight?"

They made it back home about 11:30 P.M. Keenah and the kids were already in bed, which gave Wavy the confidence to come in. Neempau and Wavy sat in the living room discussing the events of the night, while each of them held ice packs to various areas on their bodies.

"I was going to smash that guy," declared Neempau.

Wavy said, "Yeah, Cuz, you had him. Say, Cuz, I'm sorry about tonight. I thought the place would be cool. Just wanted you to get your mind off things for a bit."

"No worries, it's fine, Wavy. But what just happened exposes how bad and racist people are in this world. I've seen many like those guys before; I'm not surprised, at all. This is another reason why their Thanksgiving is so phony. I mean, what is it really teaching? Giving thanks? I tell you, Wavy-"

Neempau paused and listened to the din of George rustling through the fridge in the kitchen. He then raised his tone to ensure George would hear his words.

"As I was saying Wavy, Indians have to stick together! You know, the real Indians!"

The fridge was suddenly slammed shut and George stormed upstairs to his room.

Wavy looked as if he wanted to say something, but refrained.

Neempau bobbed his head, as if in sync with the stamping of George's feet, then let off a little chuckle. He looked at Wavy, "So, how do you feel? Can you drive home or what?"

"I'm good, Cuz, I'm good."

The thumping sound resumed. George hurried back downstairs. He had a folder full of papers in his hands, and he rushed over to Neempau, and threw them in his lap. Neempau, startled, asked, "What, what's this?"

George snapped, "It's the Nipmuc Roster, the Earle Report of 1861 and the Nipmuc Land Claims Descendants of 1888, along with the complete and original documents of my family's genealogy. As you will see, my family is on both of these documents."

Neempau's reply was awkward. "Ah, come on, I don't need to see that. Forget it."

"No! You look at it! I'm sick of you! You've been hassling me all day and I've had it! I'm just as much Nipmuc as you are! You're nothing special, you know. You think those braids and revolutionary talk makes you more Indian?"

Neempau eyes sharpened and he sat straight up.

"I'm here with a steady job, raising a family. What have you done? You haven't even lived in your own community for decades and you want to judge me? I had it rough too — you know why? It was usually from people like you, who were so mad and hateful that they tear down their own people."

"You better watch it!" Neempau shouted.

"You're no better than those idiots at the bar! You talk this rebel and revolution stuff and you've never accomplished anything! You are not your father, Neempau!"

Neempau lunged up from the couch and stared angrily at George while clenching his fists. George stood his ground as Keenah ran downstairs and shouted, "What is going on in my house?"

Neempau said, "I'm getting out of here, that's what's going on. Let's go, Wavy!"

Keenah attempted to gather more information from Neempau but he and Wavy made a hurried exit.

George told Keenah, "Don't bother. Let him go."

As they pulled out of the driveway and sped away, Keenah sadly looked out the window until the car was out of sight.

Chapter 7

Nesasuk

Wavy and Neempau made their way back to the Nipmuc Reserve. They detoured onto the back roads toward the highest point on the Reservation. They drove the car up the mountain as fast, and as far, as they could, then got out and walked to the top.

It was a cool Star-studded night. The Autumn Moon had a chalky glow from the delicate shades of thin, passing clouds that retreated over the hills.

"Man, sure good to have you back, Cuz. How ya feelin?"

Neempau rotated his shoulders and flexed his arms, "I'm good; those jerks couldn't fight. How 'bout you?"

"Never better, 'I'm right as the mail.'"

Neempau turned to Wavy with a baffled look.

"Doc Holliday – *Tombstone*?"

"Whatever you say, Wavy."

Miles off in the distance, the faint lights of the city reflected the outside world, and the place Neempau wished to escape from, but the home and fame Wavy still searched for.

Wavy retrieved three Roman candles from his car and then mounted them in the ground. As he lit them one by one, he explained, "These two I light for my boys, and this one is for you, Naomi."

The fireworks illuminated the sky with a colorful array of sparkles coupled with the cracking sound of their release. Neempau sat comfortably on the moonlit grassy hilltop, gazing thoughtfully up to the Stars.

Once the pyrotechnics were concluded, Wavy parked himself beside Neempau and the two men sat quietly, confined in their own thoughts for several minutes. Neempau finally broke the silence and asked in a soft voice, "Wavy? Why do you think people hurt each other?"

Wavy paused for a moment, cupped his hand around a lighter, lit a cigarette and said, "Wow, Cuz, I dunno. You got me on that one. Well, maybe because when people hurt, they think that if they hurt others, then they can get rid of their own pain."

Neempau nodded his head, and then did a double take at Wavy, and asked, "When did you start smoking?"

Wavy took a drag, cracked a smile, and answered, "I just started. I guess I'm trying to find new ways to hurt myself, too."

Neempau flashed a brief, subtle smile and said, "Yeah, I just don't know, anymore. Not much about anything. I came back here with a mission, and so far? I don't know. I can't even get my own sister to stop celebrating Thanksgiving. And, that George? Huh, that guy—he's crazy. You see the way he went after me in the house?"

Neempau glanced at Wavy, looking for the affirmative nod, but instead Wavy puffed on his cigarette and looked to the Earth. Neempau asked, "Hey, you get what I mean, right?"

Wavy hesitated for a moment, "I dunno, Cuz. You have been a little rugged on him."

Neempau took a sudden breath as if he was about to speak, but then Wavy quickly stated, "I'm just sayin', Cuz, I'm just sayin'."

Neempau didn't respond but his somber facial expression seemed to admit guilt.

Feeling the need to try and cheer up his cousin, Wavy slapped Neempau on the shoulder and said, "Well, wait a minute, Cuz — we got the Frogman. He's down for the cause, and so is that cutie at the Tribal Office, and those young guys we ran into. How many signatures do we have?"

Neempau smirked, and in a voice full of sarcasm said, "Okay, so we have: 'I can't make you any promises' Harriet Vickers, the Frogman, and 42 signatures. And I hope those teens are out filling up that petition I gave them."

Neempau gave Wavy a stern glance. Just as Wavy looked back, both men broke into vigorous laughter.

The thundering roll and whistle of the nearby train passing the Reservation soon filled their ears. Wavy stood up and looked out into the distance. He then asked Neempau, "So, Cuz, the night is still young — what do you wanna do?"

"Still young? It's almost one in the morning! I'm not usually up this late."

"Come on, Cuz. It's not too late; you're only 40. And what do they say? Forty is the new 30!"

Neempau chuckled. "Thirty or 40, the only thing I want to do is wake people up about Thanksgiving. I mean, come on; even if they wanna believe that whole harmonious 'Indians and Pilgrims sitting down at the table' thing, people should just ask themselves: why don't we, at least, have half of our own Country?"

Wavy threw his hands up and lit another cigarette.

Neempau continued, "They have these phony-baloney Government Agencies set up to help Indians and when we come for help, they make us feel like beggars asking for stuff that was stolen from us. This is a crazy and upside-down world, man."

Neempau paused, his voice wavered a bit, "The schools — the schools force Indian children to play dress-up for Thanksgiving, and if they don't play along, they lock them in closets and—"

Wavy suddenly turned to Neempau with a look of concern. Neempau was panting and looking to the ground. Wavy inquired, "Hey, hey, Cuz what is it, who's locked in a closet?"

Neempau sucked in a deep breath, picked his head up and said, "Nothing, nothing. Forget it. I'm fine. It's just like I said, Thanksgiving is a lie, a lie that needs to be exposed."

Wavy looked off into the distance as he took another long drag off his cigarette. He then did a side turn to Neempau, like a 1980s action hero, and said, "Cuz! I got it! I know what we have to do. Let's go."

Neempau looked puzzled, but followed Wavy's lead, nonetheless. They rushed back to the car, left the Reservation and drove North. After travelling close to an hour – first down the highway, then on back roads – they pulled into a small country 24-hour Gas and Go station.

Neempau, who was still unsure what was going on, asked, "What are we doing here? You hungry? Need some gas?"

Wavy grinned. "Nope, we're just parking here. Come on!"

As the two men began walking up the dark country road, Neempau asked suspiciously, "Wavy, where the heck are we going?"

Wavy, still maintaining his beaming smile said, "You'll see, it's about a mile up." After walking for some time, Wavy informed Neempau, "Okay, okay, right up here."

Neempau remained perplexed, for on both sides of this lonely, sparsely lit road was dense forest shrouded in low-lying fog that was devoid of homes or any other dwelling.

"Ok, there it is. Right there." Wavy whispered, pointing at a small path between the tree line on the right side of the road. Wavy signaled

Neempau to follow him like a soldier on reconnaissance. The two men followed the path which weaved through the thicket for 200 yards, then angled up another 300 yards, until the trail came to a knoll.

Wavy reached the ridge first and laid down on the moist, cold bed of leaves and pine needles in a prone position. Neempau soon followed and reluctantly did the same. Wavy peered down and pointed to the valley below and proclaimed, "There it is, Cuz."

Wavy had taken Neempau around the back to the forested side of the 'one and only' Mondo Snood's Farm Famous Turkey Farm. The ranch itself sat near a neighboring road. It was about 400 yards away from them, situated at the bottom of a flat, open field.

Wavy and Neempau looked down on the huge, tan barn from the concealed location of the misty woodland hilltop. Neempau gazed down at the turkey farm, then slowly turned his head to Wavy and asked, "Well, what we are doing here? What did you bring me out here for?"

Wavy said, "Remember what you said, Cuz? You wanna 'wake people up?' Well, this is it, Cousin, this is our first attack. We're gonna free those turkeys."

Neempau gasped and whispered, "What? Are you crazy?"

Wavy snickered and replied, "That's 'Crazy Wavy,' thank you very much. No, no, Cuz, but seriously, think about it — no turkeys, no Thanksgiving. Never mind any petition — this cuts right to the heart of the matter."

"I don't know about this," said Neempau. "This is nuts, forget it. Let's get out of here."

Neempau began to get up to leave, but Wavy pulled him back down and urgently pleaded, "Let's go for it, Cuz. You been pissed off since you got back here. I can see this whole thing has been eatin' at you. I know doing this will make you feel a whole lot better. Besides, let all these people wake up to see their symbol of Thanksgiving is gone. This will give them something to think about, for sure."

After a moment of reflection, a cunning smile spreading on Neempau's face revealed that the idea was beginning to take hold. "You know what's funny, Wavy?" Neempau said in a more upbeat tone, "I bet there wasn't even turkey at the fabled Thanksgiving dinner of 1621- let's do it."

"Yes!" Wavy said excitedly before lowering his voice. "Okay, Cuz, this is what we have to do: We gotta get across that field and get down to that barn; that's where all those turkeys are. See that big house off to the left? That's where Mondo Snood lives. Looks like all the lights are off down there. I can't really see because of the fog, but all we gotta do is get to the barn, swing open those doors, and out comes the turkeys."

The two men began to slowly, and stealthily, come down the hill and approached the side of the barn. Along the way, Wavy took a misstep and slid down. He skidded down to the bottom, on his side, leaving a track of muck and debris along the side of his body. Wavy wanted to yell out in pain, but managed to hold in the yelp.

Neempau rushed to help him up, and whispered, "Shh! Be careful-you're gonna get us busted!"

Once Wavy got up, he wiped himself off. He then looked at his muddy palms curiously. Following that, he took some of the mud and made lines across his face. Neempau raised his eyebrows and shook his head as Wavy continued applying the earth tones. Neempau abruptly elbowed him in the side, causing him to stop the artwork and refocus on the task at hand.

Through the darkness and misty haze, the two men eyed the big barn. They got into a crouched position. Quickly and quietly, they ran towards the farmhouse. They made it to the barn undetected and breathed a sigh of relief. They crept around to the front and squatted down underneath the large swinging doors. Neempau and Wavy took a deep breath and gave each other a successful look. Just as they were exchanging a victorious fist bump, the men were startled by a bellowing Hoot owl nearby. They started to shout but hastily calmed themselves as they prompted each other to be quiet.

The two took a breath and then, on a count of three, rose in-sync and pulled on the door. The door did not open. They tugged again with no result. They shuddered in disappointment while some clucking and gobbling began to stir from the inside of the barn.

"Uh, man. It's locked," Neempau grumbled.

"No worries, Cuz. Come on, let's try the other end."

They snuck around to the other end of the barn and tried their luck there. They found that the door on that side was bolted, too.

Neempau uttered in disappointment, "Uh, I knew it. Forget it, let's get out of here."

Wavy began to look at the barn, up and down, and all around, searching for a way in. He then pointed to a small window and whispered, "Hey Cuz, right there. See that window? If you boost me up there, I can squeeze in and open it up from the inside."

Neempau hesitated momentarily, but eventually gave in. He bent down to let Wavy get on his shoulders. After a few moans, strains, and wobbles, he got his footing and lined Wavy up under the window. In a tense voice, Neempau said, "Hurry up, get in there!"

Wavy managed to open the window and peeked in. He shouted, "Holy moly, that's a lot of turkeys!"

"Keep it down, just go," Neempau said with a groan.

Wavy said, "And you know what, Cuz? That Mondo guy wasn't kiddin. These snoods are huge."

"Just get in there!"

Wavy's moment of awe subsided and he crawled through. He scurried and zigzagged, between the sea of turkeys, and unlatched the doors where Neempau was waiting on the other side. The door was now wide open. The turkeys were gobbling and scampering around but not leaving the barn. The men tried shooing the birds, but they were unsuccessful.

"Uh, they won't leave," said Neempau. "Of course, this is where the food is," he added in a distressed tone.

Wavy smiled and nodded, lit a cigarette and stated, "No worries, Cuz, Wavy is on the job."

Wavy rushed back outside to the edge of the barn. He returned inside holding two large carved pumpkins that had been sitting by the door. He placed the pumpkins in the center of the barn and removed their tops. He took another drag of his smoke and unzipped his coat. He gave Neempau an odd little grin and asked, "Say, Cuz, did you ever see that movie called Red Skin?"

Neempau said, "Huh?"

Wavy continued to speak as he unloaded an arsenal of cherry bombs and firecrackers in the pumpkins, "It's funny, you know, Cuz — I guess in 1929, by painting Richard Dix red, he became an instant Indian. Add some red face paint, and voilà, you have Wingfoot. If I was around back then, I would'a had that part. And he would have been Turkeyfoot," he said with a laugh.

Instead of giving his full attention to Wavy's words, Neempau was nervously watching him load explosives into the pumpkins. Neempau then uttered, "Uh, Wavy, I know you're not gonna—"

Wavy replied, "And let me see if I can remember — How does that song go? Oh yeah," he went on in a musical tone, "Redskin, Redskin, let us return, la la la!"

Wavy paused for a moment, pulled out his lighter and leaned down to the pumpkins and sang, "'Redskin, Redskin, - let- us –return; where –bright- twilight- welcome- fires- BURN! Neempau! Run!"

The men made a fast break for the door. A series of vicious explosions erupted, creating loud booming noises inside the barn. This was quickly followed by a massive, and chaotic exodus, of close to 2,000 gobbling and yelping turkeys making their way out of the huge barn.

Wavy and Neempau ran back up the hill at top speed, but were surpassed by hundreds of fowl charging into the woods and the nearby marsh. The sound of yelping dogs was heard off in the distance as the men retreated back to their hidden position at the top of the hill. When they peered back, they noticed all the lights were on at Mondo Snood's home. To their satisfaction, they also saw that every single turkey had made a clean getaway and vanished into the night. They gave each other a high-five and took off back through the brush. As they made it back to the road, they laughed and jostled each other.

Neempau shouted, "Oh man! That was something, let them stuff that!"

Wavy threw a few punches in the air, then made the peace sign with two fingers and replied, "I told ya, Cuz. Now those are some free birds!"

"Yes, yes they are," Neempau said with a grin, "Alright; let's hurry back to the car."

"For sure, Cuz! Say, Cuz did you know that the Pilgrims are on the 10,000-dollar bill?"

Neempau replied, "Huh? No, no I didn't. You serious?"

Wavy laughed and said, "Yeah, yeah, they sure are. I think us, Indians, are on what? A few different one-dollar coins? Oh, and we have that old Indianhead nickel. You got me thinking, Cuz, we oughta' do something about that, too."

Neempau chuckled. "Right on, Wavy, but let's focus on one thing at a time. I sure do hear ya, though. The White man sure loves to put all his presidents on his money."

Wavy came back with, "Well, maybe there should be a Chief from every Tribe on our money instead."

"Now you're thinkin', Wavy."

Just as the pair came within view of the 24-hour Gas-n-Go Mart, Wavy fervently let loose a loud shriek and cried, "My Mustang! Where's my car?"

They both jetted to the empty parking lot in the front of the store, and stood there, with identical expressions of dismay. They bolted inside to question the clerk who claimed he hadn't seen anything. When they returned outside, Wavy called the police. Neempau anxiously paced around the parking lot and looked, both ways, down the road. After several moments on the phone with the cops, Wavy shuffled to the edge of the road and slumped to the ground.

Neempau ran over to him and asked, "Hey Wavy, what's up? Are they coming? What's wrong? What did they say?"

Wavy slowly lifted his head and replied, his voice little more than a dragging whisper, "It's not stolen, Cuz."

"Huh? What do you mean it's not stolen? Where—?"

"It's been repossessed, Cuz. They came and took it."

Neempau jolted. "But how, why? You told me you just got the car five months ago."

Wavy just shook his head.

"You made your payments, right?" Neempau asked.

Wavy hesitated then said, "Well, Cuz, I missed a few payments."

"How many?"

Wavy replied slowly, his voice timid, "Uh, four."

"Ooh man! Why you stupid—" said Neempau, cutting himself off. "Do you have any idea how far away from home we are? Damn! How did they find you way up here anyway?"

"Aaaw, Cuz. All these new cars, they got that GPS tracking system crap in them. Can't really hide anywhere like the old days. I— I just didn't have the money."

"Money? Back when we got the flat tire, you called your insurance company. What did they tell you? You knew they were gonna take it, didn't ya? Didn't ya?"

Wavy covered his face with his hands.

Neempau circled him like shark around its prey, "Urg! Keenah was right! You haven't been going to work. You and your duct tape dreams and, and Hollywood nonsense! What's the matter with you? Man! Damn, we're screwed—plus, the petitions were in the car!"

"I'm sorry, Cuz," Wavy sadly responded as he rubbed his eyes. "Really, I'm sorry."

"Sorry? You're sorry, all right. Here we are in the middle of nowhere, 50 miles from home, and you're sorry?"

Wavy held his head in his lap and remained silent through the castigation.

Neempau stormed across the road and plopped down under a maple tree. Neempau peered up at the Stars and took a deep breath. After a few minutes, he looked across the empty road. Wavy sat dejectedly, his body hunched under the dim light of the parking lot. However, Neempau didn't see his cousin — he saw himself, back in fourth grade.

Neempau jumped up and walked toward him. He placed his arm around Wavy's shoulder and said, "Hey man, forget about it. Other than the part that we have to walk, you did good tonight."

105

As Wavy raised his head, Neempau gave him a smile as if to say 'it's okay.'

Wavy chuckled and then both men broke into laughter.

"We better get going," said Neempau. "We might just make it home by morning."

The two set off down the long, winding, and isolated road, where a car, or two, would pass by every 15 to 20 minutes. After walking close to five miles, Wavy's leg was beginning to cause him pain on the side he fell on, back at Mondo's farm. He, reluctantly, resorted to hitchhiking; throwing the thumbs up on the rare occasion a vehicle passed by, while limping more, and more, as their trek continued.

Neempau took notice of his agony and asked, "Hey Wavy, do you remember our Woodland Stompdance song?"

Wavy chuckled and said, "Of course, Cuz. I mean, I ain't been to a pow wow in ages, but I think I still know it."

Neempau started off the traditional song with, "Way-Hey -Ya-Hey!"

Wavy followed the cadence, "Way –Hey – Ya- Hey!"

"Yo-Ho-Hey –Yah!"

Wavy repeated in kind, "Yo-Ho-Hey –Yah!"

The song harmonized in a lead-and-chorus-style tempo. Next, the vocals increased as the octave went lower, then the lyrics decreased as the chants escalated. Soon enough, Wavy had forgotten about his pain, as the Nipmuc men sang their song.

After they finished singing, Neempau said, "Hey, Wavy."

"Yeah, Cuz?"

"You're right, Harriet is cute."

Wavy laughed. "Aye. I told ya."

"Yeah, but you know, I was seeing someone. I left kind of suddenly. I don't know, it just never seems to work out. I've got too much on my mind."

Wavy stopped walking for a moment, patted Neempau on the back and said, "Now Cuz, how can anybody have too much on their mind when it comes to woman?"

Neempau smirked and said, "Let's go, Wavy."

After walking another three miles, they spotted a car coming their way. It was an older model SUV with some rust stains on the side and a dent on the door. Wavy, halfheartedly, stuck his thumb up as the vehicle went by. To their surprise, it slowed down. It came to a halt about 300 feet ahead of them, with the car still running. As Neempau and Wavy looked to the car with hopeful eyes; nobody got out. It remained in a static position save for the fumes from the exhaust, rising through the light mist, above the cracked brake light.

Neempau shouted over to the car, "Hello!" He got no response. He turned to Wavy with a look of doubt. To their surprise, both passenger and driver's doors opened simultaneously, and two men emerged from the SUV. As the two men approached them, Wavy and Neempau were stunned to see that it was Jasper and Chet, the guys they had the scuffle with at The Cue & Sip. To make things worse, two other men also exited the truck and followed closely behind Jasper and Chet. They were all holding something in their hands.

Jasper coldly eyed Neempau and Wavy. With a devilish grin he said, "My, my, my, sweet baby, Jesus. You know what, Chet? It's only a few days till Thanksgiving, but it looks like we got ourselves an early Christmas present."

"Mm-mm" said Chet, with a cigarette hanging off the tip of his lip. "Why yes, I think we do."

Jasper gawked at Wavy and said, "Hey! God dang, what is that on your face, boy? Looks like you rubbed your face in a cow pie."

Wavy hastily wiped the mud from his cheeks that he had applied earlier.

"Hah! You called it, Chet, you called it. Hot dang! Fire-dancing mud boys!" Jasper shouted, "We got some unfinished business. You mud boys are in a lot of trouble."

Chet said to the other guys with them, "Hey Nudder, Lewis, these are the ones! It's them, all right. They think they can put their filthy hands on us and get away with it?"

Chet and Jasper were holding baseball bats. Nudder was carrying a 12-inch screwdriver in one hand and a fifth of whisky in the other. Lewis approached wielding a lug wrench.

As Chet began to walk closer to Neempau, he rested the bat over his left shoulder. He took a long drag off his cigarette and then flicked it towards Neempau's face. Neempau turned his head, avoiding the cigarette, and said, "No thanks, I don't smoke."

"Oh no?" Nudder asked, "I thought you boys love to make smoke signals." The four men laughed.

They surrounded Wavy and Neempau. Nudder took a large swallow of whisky then smashed the bottle on the side of the road.

"That's gonna be your face!" Nudder shouted.

"You tell'm Nudder!" Lewis said, as he clenched the lug wrench tight.

"Nudder? What kind of name is that?" Wavy asked. "I don't think your parents liked you. They must have wanted a 'Nudder' child."

Nudder scowled, pointed at Wavy with the screwdriver and shouted, "You watch your stinkin mouth! Who the hell do you think you are?"

Chet said, "Don't you worry about it Nudder, let's do it!"

As the men moved in for the kill, Wavy turned to Neempau, and with an unsteady laugh said, "Hey Cuz, in all the good movies, the hero dies, right?" He then shouted, "Hey, all you punks! I bet you all hit like little girls. Come and get me!"

Wavy shut his eyes tight and stood still.

Neempau yelled, "Wavy, no!"

"Just get out of here, Cuz!"

"No! I am not leavin' you, Wavy!"

"Aww, ain't this sweet?" said Chet. "Huh, it doesn't matter, though; both of you, long-haired, canoe-jockeys, are about to die!"

Just as the men were lunging to attack, a car came blazing down the road. It screeched to a halt in front of the scene. All the action paused due to the new arrival. The person driving was concealed because of his high beam lights shining in their faces.

The driver's-side door flew open and a man wearing a long trench coat stepped out into view. It was Neempaus' brother in-law George. There seemed to be something large and concealed under his trench coat.

George shouted, in a loud and sharp tone, to the assailants, "Listen up and listen good. Under my coat is a fully-automatic shotgun and if you thugs don't get the hell out of here, I'm gonna start shooting!"

Jasper smirked and said, "Never even heard of one of those. We don't even know if that is a gun, or not!"

George shouted back, "I tell you what, if I have to take this out of my coat, I'm gonna use it. You don't believe it's a gun, huh? This is your last warning. I'm gonna count to three. If you scum are still here when I'm done, I'm going squeeze the trigger and not let go until all the bullets are gone, and I'm going to start with you, Mister 'I don't think it's a gun!'— One!" The four men stared at each other nervously. "Two!" George gave motion, as if he were about to open his coat.

Before George could finish his count, the four men fled back to their truck with Jasper leading the way. They dove into their seats and before they could get the doors shut, Jasper hit the accelerator and burned rubber down the road.

Wavy chased the truck for a few steps and yelled, "And don't come back!"

Wavy turned back to George, "Holy, Cuz! It's so good to see you! What are you doin' out here? How did you find us?"

George replied, "Well, Keenah told me not to let her brother out my sight. So, after you guys left, I followed you to the Rez. Then, I trailed you two up here to a store about 10 miles back. I saw your car sitting at the parking lot for a while, so I left. I was just coming back through and saw the car was gone and figured you guys had left. Wait, where is the car? And what are you guys doing up here, anyway? And Wavy? On your face, is that mud? What— what is going on?"

"Oh George, let's just get out of here, we'll tell you all about it," said Neempau, exhaustedly, "on the way home."

As the men wearily got into George's car, Neempau asked, "So, George, I didn't know you had an automatic shotgun?"

Just before George sat down, he said, "Automatic shotgun? I hate guns. Never owned one. I just made that up on the spot. This is my 'automatic shotgun.'"

George pulled out his daughter's Lacrosse stick from under his coat, and tossed in the back seat.

The men released a worn-down, but joyful, chuckle.

As they drove off, Wavy declared, "Nice move, Cuz. Nice move."

The drive home was somber and reflective. Neempau and Wavy neglected to tell George the real reason they were so far away from home. However, after George took a couple of curious whiffs, he asked, "Say, have you guys been near a farm, or something?"

They were both silent for a moment, then Neempau said, "No—I mean—there's farms all around here, I guess."

Once back on Nipmuc land, George dropped Wavy off at his place and they proceeded home.

Now that Wavy was out the car; Neempau made an attempt of contrition and said, "Say, uh, George, I just wanted to—"

George stopped him. "It's fine. It's fine."

That was the end of their conversation for the rest of the trip. When they finally arrived home, Neempau went straight to the bed.

Chapter 8

Shwosuk

The next day, Neempau was awakened by his nephew, Robert. The teenage boy tugged on the shoulder of his uncle, who was lying down in his bed, facing the powder-blue wallpaper. After a third, and a more robust, shove, Neempau turned in his direction. While rubbing his face and clearing his eyes, Neempau asked in a groggy voice, "Hey what — what's up? What time is it?"

"It's 10 A.M.," said Robert. "I learned in school that 'A.M.' means 'ante meridiem,' which is Latin for 'before noon.'"

Neempau replied in a tired tone, "Oh. That's nice, Robert. Hey, tomorrow is the start of the four-day Harvest Moon Ceremony. The Sacred Fire will be lit at dawn, at the Sunrise Ceremony. I want all of you guys to go. I just hope your folks don't give me a hard time."

Robert replied, "Yeah, I wanna go. Uncle Neempau, I've been thinkin' about that cool story you told me and Silvia and, well, now I've been thinkin' a lot about Thanksgiving, like never before. I learn a lot of stuff in school, like the Pantheon of the Greek gods, but they never talk about Thanksgiving like you did. I wanna know more about Massasoit and all those other Indians around here, especially our Nipmuc people. Why doesn't the school teach about us?"

Neempau sat up on the edge, "That's good, kid. Always ask questions. Massasoit? He was a great leader — somebody should have put him on the 10,000-dollar bill. Also, I bet you didn't know that, in his later years, he joined with his Nipmuc people of Quaboag.

So, he's our family, too. That was also around the time he changed his name to 'Ousamequin,' which means Yellow Feather. Massasoit had a great vision of peace and unity of all peoples."

Neempau began undoing his bed-head braids as he went on, "That's why he didn't attack the Pilgrims; he knew building friendship is far better than creating enemies. But of course, the Puritans, Pilgrims — you know, the first illegal aliens — spread like roaches in a large city. They didn't care about peace; they only cared about what they could take. Our people began to die in large numbers from their diseases. They forced their laws and religion on us too."

Robert frowned and tapped on the dresser.

"Massasoit's son, whose name was 'Metacom,' but was called King Phillip by the Whites, would take over as Chief. Eventually, when the Whites couldn't steal enough land, kill enough Indians, and force our people to give up our spirituality, a big war broke out, known as the King Phillip's War."

"Whoa, never heard of that. When did it happen?" Robert asked.

"It was in 1675. All the Tribes of the East were involved, but when they attacked King Phillip, the first place he came to for help was Nipmuc land. This is where the great leaders of our past, like: Mattawamp, Monoco, Matoonas, Sagamore Sam, and many, many others, fought for our freedom to be who we are. Especially Mattawamp. They say he was the bravest and smartest Chief of them all. Another one of our relatives was, James the Printer, from Hassanamesit. He was famous for being one of the first Indians to translate the King James Bible into our Native language."

Robert replied in amazement, "Bible? Wicked cool!"

"And it doesn't stop there, my little Nephew. You come from people who studied the Stars and understood the planets. They were

114

skillful in agriculture, horticulture, ecology, and most of all, a connection with all living things."

"What's horticulture?"

"Oh, that has to do with growing food in a smart way. We contributed hundreds of foods and medicines, including the cultivation of corn, beans, and squash. We call it the Three Sisters."

"Wow," Robert said, "Maybe if my school taught us all that, I would pay attention more, and mom won't be mad and sayin' I don't care about school. Uncle, what school did you learn all this?"

Neempau's body shifted downward as he went silent and stared at the hard wood floor.

With a puzzled look Robert asked, "What school, Uncle?"

Neempau shook off the catatonic spell, cleared his throat and uttered, "I didn't learn any of that in school. I had to find the books and history that 'school' didn't want me to see. But don't you worry, I'm gonna show you some good books to read."

"Thanks Uncle."

"Okay, Robert, I'll talk with you some more later. I need to take a shower."

As Neempau headed for the bath, Robert took off outside on his bike. Once Neempau finished his shower, his sister called from the other room. "Hey Neempau pick up the phone, it's for you!"

"Hello?"

A soft voice said, "Hey, uh, just wanted to call. Make sure you're ok."

"Hi, Gladys. Yeah, yeah, I'm fine. Thanks for asking."

"Look, I know why you went back. I saw the letter denying the appeal."

After a brief pause, Neempau said, "Let me tell you why I am here. I'm going to end Thanksgiving."

"What? Neempau, what are you talking about? How are you supposed to do that?"

"With a petition."

" Huh, petition?"

"Yes, that's right. I already have a couple thousand signatures, and the list is growing."

"Well, I know this appeal denial must really have you upset. I don't even know how many years you've been trying to sue the State for your father's death."

Neempau cleared his throat; his voice trembled as he said, "Gladys, Gladys. I don't want to talk about this right now. I—"

"Neempau, I need to tell you something, before you hear it from someone else."

"Go on."

"I've been talking to my ex–husband. We're getting back together. I just wanted you to—"

"Oh, that's— that's good. Good for you." Neempau said.

"I was always hoping things between you and I could be more, but I know you're—"

"No, No I, I understand, that's fine. Well, listen, I need to go, okay? Take care."

"But Neempau, we're still frien—"

Neempau hung up the phone and held his face in his hands. He took a deep breath and rubbed his eyes before he went down stairs for some breakfast.

He expected his sister to ask about the quarrel last night, but as he walked toward the kitchen, he saw that she was preoccupied watching the morning news.

"We have a breaking news story from WNDN channel 18 this morning, ladies and gentlemen! It seems that someone is trying to knock the stuffing out of Thanksgiving. Last night at Mondo Snood's Farm Famous Turkeys, a group of bandits or maybe crazed maniacs, decided to let loose every single turkey! It is estimated that there are over 2,000 birds at large, somewhere in the wilderness of Massachusetts. Mr. Snood is asking for the public's help. He says, and I quote, 'Thank you to all my loyal customers over the years, but now I need your help. Please, if you see a turkey with a huge snood, please call us right away at: 1-800- MY-SNOOD, thank you.' We will keep you updated as this story develops."

Keenah shook her head and said, "Oh my God. Can you believe that? What kind of idiots would do such a thing?"

Neempau was using the refrigerator door for concealment as he pretended to rummage inside looking for the milk. Under his breath he excitedly whispered, "Yes!" as he pumped his fist in the air. He then put on a look of indifference and said, "Aw that's nothing, probably a blessing in disguise. Why should all those poor birds be butchered every November in some mass execution? Hey, they're free now. Besides, Sis, why don't you guys just forget Thanksgiving this year? Your kids are okay with it. And, they wanna go to the lighting of the Sacred Fire at dawn tomorrow."

Silvia rushed in the kitchen grabbed a bottled water and declared, "That's right, Mom. We wanna go tomorrow. I'll see you old folks later. Fredrick and I are going over to the school track for a run. Gotta stay in shape for next season. Bye-bye, Uncle Neempau."

Keenah sighed, then sneered, and said, "Look, Big Brother, we've had this talk before. What do you want from me? I know we didn't have Thanksgiving growing up, and I know why. I heard all the stories; I was there, too. But I've worked hard to give my kids a good life and we don't see anything wrong with celebrating. This isn't about the Mayflower. It's about our family being happy. I told you, I can't live the life of Mom and Dad."

Neempau jumped in and stated, "Well. that's fine, Sis, but why don't you at least tell your kids the truth? They don't know anything about the true history of our people."

"Tell them what, Neempau? What truth? That the White people have tried to exterminate us since they got off the boat? How they almost killed us off with their diseases, slavery, and laws, saying that we're not even human? Huh? Then what? Have them drop out of school and march on Washington to take our Country back?"

"Yes, that would be a good start."

Keenah laughed sarcastically. "Oh Neempau, just what are you really trying to do, Big Brother? You really think after few centuries of Thanksgiving, that you're going to change it? The world is not like you think it is."

Neempau replied, "Let me ask you this, Sis: what do you believe in?"

She paused for a moment, then walked to the living room and sat down on the couch. Shortly thereafter, Neempau followed and sat beside her. They both had a look of fatigue and gazed forward in silence.

Keenah turned to her brother and said, "Okay, look, I do think it would be good idea if we all go to the Sunrise Ceremony tomorrow, but we're still having our traditional get-together called 'Thanksgiving.' I'm just ticked off now because we can't get our farm fresh turkey from Snood's, like we do every year. Thanks to some morons, now I'm going to have to buy from the supermarket."

"Yup, that's really too bad, just awful," said Neempau.

"Listen, George is at work and I'm heading out to my job in a half hour. Could you go to the supermarket and get us a 20-pound turkey? You can drop me off and take my car."

"What?!" Neempau winced, looked to the ceiling, cleared his throat, and replied with a nervous smile, "Uh Sis, I don't think I could—"

"Hey come on," said Keenah. "I'm not asking you to celebrate, or even eat it. Just go down there and get a turkey for your sister."

Neempau couldn't erase his smirk, as he shook his head and laughed under his breath. Keenah took notice, threw her hands up, rose from the sofa and said, "I know, never mind, it was silly to ask you—"

"Okay, okay, I'll go!" blurted Neempau.

Keenah softly smiled and said, "Yeah, that's my bro. By the way, I'm happy to see you and George are getting along."

Neempau sneered and opened his mouth to comment, but Keenah quickly said, "Nuh-uh. I don't want to hear it. You came back with him and that's a good beginning. Okay, I've gotta get ready. I'll be down in 10."

Shortly afterwards, the siblings were on their way. The hospital where Keenah worked was located by the city. As they drove along the route, it took them past their old elementary school. Unlike yesterday, Neempau was more reserved and in control of his feelings as he beheld the building. In a calm voice he said to Keenah, "Hey Sis, do you remember Ms. Nelson?"

Keenah replied, "Huh- you kiddin? How could I forget? Why?"

"Oh, nothing," said Neempau. "Just wondering what happened to her."

"Geez I don't know, but I do know the year I graduated, when you, *unfortunately,* had already dropped out, she had left the school. They say she sold her house and just left."

Neempau simply nodded and gazed off in the distance.

Keenah sorrowfully glanced at her brother and softly said, "You know, our parents were always proud of you."

Neempau quickly replied, "What?"

"Um, nothing," said Keenah. "It's a nice day out."

As the drive proceeded, Keenah began discussing the pains and pleasures of being a nurse, and how some staff members work harder than others.

She jokingly, but with a stern edge, pointed out, "Why do some old men think they can just grab on a nurse's body anywhere they feel like?"

Keenah chuckled. "I'm telling ya, Big Brother, you or George better never end up like that, bothering some poor nurse. I'll go on the warpath."

Neempau replied, "Very funny, Sis."

They pulled into the employee entrance and Neempau took the wheel. Just before Keenah entered the building she shouted back, "Don't forget! A 20-pound turkey! Thanksgiving is only four days away!"

Neempau grimaced, then made a half smile as he waved to his sister.

While on his way to the supermarket, Neempau made a detour to the Reservation to take Wavy along with him. He pulled up to the small, one-bedroom, apartment and knocked on his door. After several thumps, Wavy finally came and opened the door. He looked as though he had just gotten out of bed. His hair was unkempt and he was wearing a black T-shirt with a green marijuana leaf on front. He had a brown sock on one foot and a black one on the other. There were a few tiny burn holes in the large, white boxers he was wearing.

His place was modest and messy. Other than the picture of his ex-wife and children, his apartment walls were covered in old movie posters: *The Bridge on the River Kwai, Geronimo, Star Wars, Tombstone,* and many other movies, from different eras and genres.

With a sullen tone, Wavy said, "Hey Cuz, come on in. I am grounded. No freakin' car."

He then walked over to the old couch, plopped down and began to roll a joint.

Neempau said, "Yeah, I'm sorry about your car, man. We had quite the night. Well, you're not going to believe where I'm heading—"

"Hey Cuz, check this poster out over here. This is from that 1936 flick, *The Petrified Forest.* Man, I just love that Villon poem at the end. How's it go?

'You shall be always wholly till I die;
And in my right against all bitter things,
Sweet laurel with fresh rose its force shall try;
Seeing reason wills not that I cast love by
Nor here with reason shall I chide or fret
Nor cease to serve, but serve more constantly;
This is the end for which we twain are met.'

Yeah, yeah. I like that, Cuz. Man, if Naomi heard that one—"

Neempau blurted in, "Wavy- What are you talking about? I want you to—"

Wavy quickly said, "Hey Cuz, did you know Bette Davis is from Massachusetts? That's right, baby — Nipmuc land." Wavy looked down at his lap, "Damn, I'm runnin' out of rolling papers."

With a puzzled look, Neempau said, "Hey, uh, yeah. That's all cool, but get dressed, I want you to come to the supermarket with me. I gotta buy my sister a turkey, of all things. I guess we should have thought about all the grocery store birds."

Wavy was preoccupied working his hand in between the sofa searching for something as Neempau went on, "Normally, I wouldn't even dream of buying a damn turkey, but they are coming to Sunrise Ceremony tomorrow, so the way I see it, I still have time to change her mind. Come on and get dressed, man."

With a weary expression, Wavy said, "I'm sorry Cuz, I ain't up to it. You go ahead. I gotta figure out some things."

Neempau looked down at Wavy rolling another joint. He then looked up at the large poster of Steve McQueen and Dustin Hoffman. It was from the 1973 film, *Papillion*.

"Hey, uh, you alright?" asked Neempau. "Losing a car isn't the end of the world— and we can make more petitions."

Wavy said, "Yeah, I know, Cuz, I know. Anyways, you go ahead; tell my dad 'hello' when you see him at the ceremony tomorrow."

Neempau glared with concern and said, "Uh, okay. Alright. Just call me if you need anything; I got my sister's car."

After an exchange of handshakes and pats on the back, Neempau set off for the market.

He arrived at the densely-occupied parking lot of the grocery store. He had to maneuver around three times before locating a spot. It was far in the back, which he did not mind. Once he exited the car, an uncomfortable strained look came over his face. There were scores of people zipping to, and from, the store gathering their holiday food, while Neempau strolled forward.

Outside the main entrance was like a non-profit bazaar. The first two booths were selling pies and T-shirts, for local charities. The third was retailing cookies for the local high school's annual "Pumpkin Bowl" football game. Down at the end, a man was ringing a bell and collecting donations for the homeless. Once inside, Neempau realized the place was much larger than it appeared. All his senses were bombarded with a potpourri of smell, colors, and shapes. All throughout the store, the song "Over the River and Through the Woods," was playing to an almost harmonic tempo, which seemed to encourage shopping.

Neempau moved carefully from aisle to aisle in order to avoid a collision with the multitude of consumers. Getting to the meat section was like trying to cross the street in New York, during rush-hour traffic. From his vantage point, he could not even see the selection of poultry. It was concealed behind a wall of bodies inching their way onward. All while he stood there, he was inundated with the song:

'Over the river, and through the woods,
To Grandfather's house we go;
The horse knows the way to carry the sleigh
Through the white and drifted snow—!'

There was an abrupt interruption of the musical by the store manager, "Good afternoon, shoppers: We just want to inform all of our customers that due to Mondo Snood's turkey shortage, we will only have a limited supply so, please, shop early! Happy Thanksgiving to all!"

Then it was back to the jingle;

'Over the river, and through the woods,
To Grandfather's house away!
We would not stop for doll or top,
For this is Thanksgiving Day...'

After being overtaken by frustration, and the song, Neempau spied a sign that read, 'Food Court.' He escaped the meat frenzy, for a timeout, and followed the arrow leading to some coffee. Suddenly, like a lucid nightmare, Neempau was grabbed by a man in a Pilgrim costume. He was complete with stockings, garters, breeches, doublet, ruff, and, of course, his felt steeple hat. The Pilgrim seemed in distress and before Neempau could get a word out, the Pilgrim fellow said, "Oh my god! Finally, you're here! Come, come quick!"

Before Neempau could get a grip on the moment, the Pilgrim guided him to a side door leading to a back room. Next he pointed to an Indian costume and said, "Okay, there it is, put it on. We don't have much time; they only gave us a 60-minute slot to do everything."

Neempau, still in shock, replied with a bitter chuckle, "What the hell are you talking about, man? You got the wrong—"

"Yeah, yeah sure. I get it," he interrupted, in a snide tone, "You're on Indian time, right- right." He laughed, "But, they're paying us by the hour, so get your butt in gear."

Neempau cut his eyes at the man and stared in silence.

The Pilgrim brought Neempau's attention back to the door, then pointed off to the left and stated, "Look over there. That's where we set up."

The man was showing Neempau a mock 1621 Colonial home and Indian Wetu set up in the supermarket food-court area. The props were made from plastic and fiberglass and were brought in as a sales stunt for the holidays. A 'Pilgrim' and 'Indian' were hired to stand in front of the fake site and take photos with the customers. However, it seemed the 'Indian' didn't show up. Once the man informed Neempau of his 'assignment,' he bitterly mumbled, "You've got to be kidding."

Neempau began to sweat, and he could hear his sprinting heartbeat pounding between his own ears. The Pilgrim continued to speak to Neempau, but it was inaudible to him. Neempau felt dizzy, and as if he were underwater. While Neempau gazed at the artificial home and Wetu, the Pilgrim was trying to put the imitation buckskin costume in his hands.

Then, like the sudden breaking of a dam, Neempau overflowed all over the Pilgrim. He snatched him by the doublet, hurled him around, and then threw him, causing him to crash into a pallet of Quaker oatmeal. The dazed man flailed about, amidst a blizzard of swirling oats unfurled from the busted canisters.

Neempau shouted, "Hey! Hey! What the hell did I tell you?"

The man screamed back "Aaarg! Help! Help! He's a maniac!"

"Maniac? I'll show you a maniac!"

Neempau burst out of the backroom and charged at the mock village. He immediately began to rip the set apart. Shoppers looked on in dismay while Neempau completely destroyed both, the Wetu, and the Colonial home.

A voice from the crowd shrieked, "Security! Security!"

At that moment Neempau came to his senses. While panting heavily and with look of distress, he pointed to the destruction, "This crap is not who we are!" shouted Neempau. "It's just like how your Thanksgiving is, not who you are. When are you people gonna wake up?" Neempau looked around, then quickly walked off.

He left the store without purchasing the turkey. Once outside, he paused and leaned over holding himself at the knee; much like a basketball player catching his breath after a run to the hoop. He peeked back to see if he was being followed. He then took the long walk back to his sister's car.

Just as Neempau was about to unlock the car door, he heard a soft female voice that said, "Pssst! Hey there, sweetie."

Instead of immediately turning around, he simply paused for a moment. The soft voice said, "Psst-Psst. You there. Hey, handsome."

Neempau turned his head to the voice and noticed a gorgeous, extra plus-sized, woman sitting in a tiny, compact car. She had pretty glowing skin, dazzling green eyes, and was sporting a small diamond nose ring. She had full lips, which were accented with a red gloss, and a black outline. She wore neon-purple hoop earrings, which matched the purple streak in her shoulder-length, dark hair. Over her thin, peach v-neck, she wore a petite, light-brown sheepskin coat, which allowed her to display her best attributes.

The woman said, "Hey there, cutie. That's right, I'm talking to you, with the long braids."

Neempau forced a smile in her direction but he was in no mood for chit-chat, following his ordeal in the store. He waved to her and resumed putting the key in the door.

The woman quickly shouted, "Hey, hey, don't leave! Come over here!"

Neempau made a forced grin, took a deep breath and walked over to her little car.

The woman said in a very smooth voice, "I'm glad you came over here. I know it was a little rough in there, but I got something that can really, really make you happy. And it won't cost you much."

The woman gazed intensely into Neempau's eyes, and he was compelled to do the same. Once she saw that she had his full attention, she slowly began to shift her eyes down towards her lap.

Neempau strained his neck for a moment as if caught by a magnetic force as he tried to move. He regained his composure quickly and fell back two steps away from the vehicle.

"Whoa-whoa," he uttered, "look, I'm not that kind of a guy."

The woman smiled and looked at him up and down. "You know, you can go to jail for this type of stuff," he said. "You seem like a nice person and all, but this is not the place to be doing your type of business."

With a seductive smile she responded, "Aaaw, tisk, tisk – that's too bad, cutie, but I don't make a business out of this. This is actually my first time doing it."

"Then why do it? Neempau asked, "Are you that desperate for money?"

"Well, darling, the money's nice, but when you have two big ones like this, it just makes me want to share."

Neempau gasped.

"And I know how it is; this time of year people are so desperate, so I came out here to share that with which I've been blessed. Are you sure you don't want it, honey? I'll even show them to you first."

Neempau choked on his words and said, "N-No! Hell No! What's the matter with you? I'm not gonna pay for it! Never have, and never will!"

The woman replied, "Well, okay, okay, don't be so rugged about it. Never pay for it, huh? Well, I didn't know turkeys were for free, where you come from."

Neempau did a double take. "Huh? What? T- turkeys?"

The woman reached down under her feet and picked up a huge fresh turkey and said with a sarcastic laugh, "Yeah, duh, turkey. What did you think I was talking about? I got here early today, after I saw the news about the fiasco at Snood's. I knew the birds would go fast, so I purchased two of the biggest, and best, turkeys they had. Once I realized I wouldn't need them both, I stuck around to see if someone would need one. So, when I saw you coming out empty handed, I figured you needed one, but I guess I was wrong."

Neempau quickly said, "Uh, no — I mean yes, I do! I do want the turkey! How much?"

The woman puckered her face toward Neempau, as if he gave her the creeps. She then shook her head and said, "Well, just give me 25-bucks and it's yours. Happy Thanksgiving."

Neempau smiled at her, made the cash-for-turkey exchange and said in a tense voice, "Thank you, but pardon me for not saying the Happy-whatever-whatever thing."

The woman gave Neempau an even more dismissive glance. As she drove off, she commented, "Weird, just weird. Why are all the nice-looking guys so darn weird?"

Neempau quickly got back to the house. He tossed the turkey in the fridge. He rested both hands on the kitchen countertop, shook his head and deeply exhaled. The kids and George were out so he took that time to relax and reflect on tomorrow's Sunrise Ceremony. He went to the living room and plopped down on the couch. While lying there, he spotted an old family album on the bottom bookshelf. He crawled across the living room floor, grabbed it, and returned to his supine position on the sofa.

He first came across pictures of his sister while she was pregnant. In one photo, George was giving her a hug while holding his thumbs up and making a silly smile. The humorous snapshot brought a slight grin to Neempau's face. As he flicked to the back, he saw old shots of his mom, dad, Keenah, and himself, at a Nipmuc pow-wow when he was 15 years old. The tiny smile remained, but seemed heavier than before. He softly mumbled under his breath, "Damn."

A short time later, Silvia and Robert walked in. They both shouted at once, "Hey, Uncle!" Neempau put on a big smile and quickly sat up. Silvia walked over to give her uncle a hug.

"Okay, young warriors," Neempau said cheerfully, "don't forget that we're going to the Sunrise Ceremony tomorrow, which is also the start of the four-day Harvest Moon festival. Your Nipmuc culture is very important."

Robert said, "Cool! What time do we go?"

"At Sunrise, which means we will be leaving here about 5:00 A.M.- that's five ante-meridian, right Robert?"

Robert flushed a bit, and then sneered at his sister. Silvia sat down on the couch and said, "So, Uncle Neempau, where have you been all these years? How come you don't live in Massachusetts?"

Robert said, "Hey, you don't ask a warrior where he's been. Right, Uncle?"

Neempau produced an uncomfortable smile, ruffled Roberts's hair and said, "No, Robert, that's okay."

Neempau locked his hands together and looked away in silence for a moment. He lightly sighed and said, "My life has been much different than your mom's. I'm very proud of her, though; she did a great job with you guys. Me, when I was an ironworker, I did a lot of travelling, so I could never be here much. I gave that work up some time back but—"

"Umm, hello?" said Silvia with a mocking smile. "Come on, Uncle, we're not babies. That still doesn't answer why you didn't come back. I mean, you said you don't do that anymore, right? I know, I know. It's our dad, isn't it?"

"No, No kids! It's not that, at all," Neempau quickly responded, "Please don't think that. My reasons for not living here are—well, they have nothing to do with your dad. Look, you guys are young and have a good life ahead of you. I'm just happy to be here with you guys now. Now is what matters. Tomorrow, you two are gonna take part in your first Sunrise Ceremony."

He gave Silvia a kiss on top the head and Robert a one-armed hug. Silvia and Robert smiled as they went to their rooms.

George returned home a little later from work. Neempau got up from the couch, gave him a nod and said, "I'm going to pick up Keenah."

George said, "Oh, well, she doesn't get out for another three hours, though."

Neempau replied, "Yeah, I know." Neempau left the house and returned to the Nipmuc Reservation. He drove over to Cedar Road, parked the car and walked down the path. The condemned trestle came into view. He shook his head as if just biting a lemon. His heartbeat quickened. Neempau began taking several deep breaths to calm himself. Gingerly, he maneuvered over the old bridge, that lamely stood one 150 above the swishing river. As he reached the middle point, he inhaled deeply again, then sat down on the edge.

Neempau sat there, intensely gazing down into the rushing cold waters, as the golden-orange Sun pulled itself down to the West. He stood up and shouted out across the ravine. "Why? Why did I have to say anything?"

As the evening pressed on, Neempau departed to pick up Keenah from work. Upon their return home, the entire family retired to bed in preparation for the Sunrise Ceremony.

Chapter 9

Paskoogun

It was an hour and a half before dawn; Silvia and Robert were up and eager to make the journey to the Nipmuc Reservation. George and Keenah were making final preparations to head out.

Neempau, though, was already completely dressed and waiting in the living room. Shortly afterwards, everyone was ready, and the family made their way to the ceremony. As they approached the Sacred Grounds, there were dozens of cars already parked on the edge of the road, some even up in the grass. They found a spot a little ways down the road and parked. Robert and Silvia enthusiastically jumped out of the car. George and Keenah stepped out in a more reserved fashion.

As Neempau stepped out from the vehicle, his eyes looked up to the sky. He gazed at the stellar, and mystical, blue light glowing above them. He then set his sight on the bright indigo moon, which was encircled by a vibrant, bluish-white, icy hoop.

The family strode toward the gathering, in the cool dawn, as the scent of Sweet Grass and Sage scented the air. There was also the sound of the Tribal Drum being played, creating a double beat. This represents the heartbeat of Mother Earth. The soft, rhythmic tone resonated throughout the land, like a sublime medium between Mother Earth and the Universe, bringing all life into harmony.

They exchanged handshakes, laughs, and hugs with the other Nipmuc families making their way to the Sacred Circle. Some of the people were dressed in traditional Nipmuc clothing such as warm, buckskin tops, leggings, and moccasins, while others were bundled up in boots, jeans and parkas. Regardless of what they wore, they all had equally come to honor their heritage.

Neempau observed that Harriet Vickers had come with some of her relatives, too. Harriet was wearing a wool Pendleton coat, jeans, and black boots. He walked up to her, "Hey, how you doing?" he said with a smile.

"I'm good, looking forward to the ceremony," she said, "But just so you know, I did make some calls, talked to a few council members, and—well, let's just say the idea of trying to end Thanksgiving seemed a little extreme to them."

Neempau smiled, nodded with his head down, and began to walk away. She grabbed his arm, "Wait, I know you're on to something," she said, "People have many ways of getting the message out, so don't give up, okay."

Neempau smiled and said, "Thanks for the encouragement. Oh— looks like your husband is calling you over there."

"Husband?" she laughed, "I don't have a husband. I don't even have a boyfriend. That's my cousin," she said, "I don't have time for guys, right now."

She smiled at Neempau, and left to walk with her relatives. Neempau rejoined his sister and family and headed in to the ceremony.

As they entered the path leading to the Sacred Circle, the mood became more solemn and thoughtful. Under the Arbor they took notice of the Quabbin Lake Singers, who were drumming for the occasion.

There was a line of about three dozen people standing at the edge of the entrance to the Round. At the lead, stood an elderly man, holding a large, white, eagle feather in one hand, and an abalone shell in the other. He was performing the smudging with Sage and Sweet Grass to cleanse and bless all those who are about to enter the Circle.

It was the man Neempau had longed to see, the Nipmuc Medicine Man Martin Attuck Sr., better known as Healing Otter. The 84-year-old man was thin, but sturdy, and six feet tall. His auburn tone skin was moderately wrinkled, especially above his cheeks. He had a gentle look and a soft pleasant smile that was befitting of his welcoming demeanor. His glasses perfectly matched his round face and highlighted his dark and thoughtful eyes.

Healing Otter's hair was cropped short, straight, and mostly white. He wore a red bandana around his head, which had a raven and hawk feather lashed to the back. Around his neck, was a handmade wampum necklace with three large bear claws secured to the front. He sported a natural brain-tanned coat made from moose hide. The arms were slightly fringed, and across the chest was a beaded design that was frequently seen on the Nipmuc Baskets of Antiquity.

He had on a new pair of generic jeans with a small leather bag tied to the side. As Healing Otter smudged the people, they all reached down and took a small pinch of Kinnikinnick, which is a blend of Tobacco, inner bark of the cherry tree, and bearberry roots. The mix was in a medium-sized Nipmuc basket, made from porcupine quills and split ash that sat atop a carved cedar log, just at the Sacred Circle's entrance.

When Neempau looked on at the Elder, his heart lit with joy. But all of a sudden, Neempau's smile dropped like a heavy rock falling from a cliff. He noticed that Healing Otter had some helpers. One was another Nipmuc man from the Reservation, but the other was a non-Native gentlemen. To add to his bitterness, Neempau observed several other non-Native people who had come to take part in the Sacred Sunrise Ceremony.

Neempau turned and scowled at the sight, and shook his head in aversion. However, George, Keenah, and the kids were not mindful of Neempau's scorn and waited, patiently, in line to be smudged. Robert tugged on his uncle and said, "This is pretty cool, Uncle. Thanks for talking Mom into bringing us."

Neempau didn't hear his nephew's comment. He was suspiciously scanning the scene, giving the non-Natives a hard, cold glare. As the Sacred Circle began to fill, it came Neempau's turn to be smudged.

As soon as Healing Otter set eyes on Neempau, he flashed a huge, sincere smile. The Elder slowly, but intently put out his arms to give Neempau an enormous hug. When Healing Otter spoke, it was in a slow, but steady, round cadence, as if every word was carefully thought out before it was spoken.

Healing Otter blissfully said, in an ancient and scratchy voice, "Taubotne Manitoo. Oh Neempau, my nephew, it is good to see that you are here. I have thought about you for some time now. Manitoo has brought you back home."

Neempau humbly said, "Thank you, Healing Otter. It's truly an honor to see you, too." He reached inside his coat and gifted the Elder with a small pouch of Tobacco. He then proceeded to say, "I've come home to protest Thanksgiving; the lies must end." Looking over at the non-Native participants, he added, "I have some other serious questions, too."

Healing Otter gestured with a subtle nod and smile, and slowly said, "Yes, yes, I understand. Please, my son, let us begin our ceremony. We will talk later."

The Elder smudged Neempau, along with the rest of the partakers. All of the people formed a huge circle as Healing Otter walked to center clearing. The old man took out a turtle-shell rattle and chanted an old song, as he circled the soon-to-be-lit Sacred Fire. He sat down on the Earth next to the clearing, laid out an elk-skin satchel, and then took out the Sacred Pipe.

He completed an intricate formality with the Sacred Pipe; its preparation to be awakened lasted about 20 minutes. After that, one of Healing Otter's non-Native helpers got out a small, simple cedar basket.

He came to each person and held out the small basket. Each individual recited a quiet prayer, and then put a pinch of the Kinnikinnick into the basket. The gentleman stepped over to Robert and Silvia, they happily said a prayer and added their Kinnikinnick. Keenah and George humbly submitted their offering into the basket.

When the man came around to Neempau, he was greeted with an angry scowl. The man slightly recoiled, but maintained his composure for the sake of his sacred task. After a brief moment of hesitation, Neempau, reluctantly, put his Tobacco mix into the basket. Once the helper concluded, he returned the filled vessel to Healing Otter. The Elder placed his hand over the basket and recited a prayer in the Nipmuc language. Then he moved his hand gradually through the Kinnikinnick, and took out a portion and filled the Sacred Pipe.

After that, he placed the small basket on a strip of white birch bark, which was atop the short cedar and pine logs, for the Sacred Fire. There was also a braid of Sweet Grass and a bundle of Sage, included among the wood.

Healing Otter looked up, and all around, and said with a pleasant and relaxed smile, "It is time."

Off in the distance, beyond the ridge, a robust orange blossom was opening its petals, and kindling the deep blue sky. The stirring ignited the swirling clouds, which commenced to illuminate an array of honey red, glowing brown, sapphire, and pink- yellow colors, as the new day approached. A dim silhouette of huge oaks, elms, and pines that sat atop the rolling hills, were splashed with this splendid, and mighty, brightness in between their yawning and waking limbs.

As the Quabbin Lake Singers maintained the heartbeat of Mother Earth on their drum, the Elder lit the Sacred Fire. As Healing Otter was assisted to his feet, he held the Sacred Pipe up to the sky. A long twig was placed in the flame then used to light the Pipe. The smoke from the Pipe was blown in all directions of the universe, while a sudden, but gentle wind, caressed and magnified the crackling embers of the fire; as if giving it the breathe of approval. After that, he delivered the ancient Nipmuc Morning Prayer:

Manitoo-Manitoo, Wame Masugkenuk Manitoo!
(Creator, Creator. Almighty Creator!)
Ken-Nootah-Nunnepoh-Anaquabean-Manitoo!
(Hear me; I stand before you, Great Spirit!)
Taubotne-Kuttabottomish-Newutche-Yeu Kesukok-Wunnegin-
(Thank You! I thank you for this beautiful day.)
Kuttabottomish-Newutche-Wunnanumaonk-
(I thank you for my good health.)
Nupeantam -Asekesukokish- Newutche-Wame-Ninnimissinnuog-
(I pray every day for all Human Beings.)
Nupeatam-Newutche -Paomoonk-Nesauk- Tahshe-Pometuonk-
(I pray for the future seven generations.)
Nupeantam-Newutche-Nishnoh-Oaas-Pomantog-
(I pray for all the living creatures.)
Nupeantam -Newutche-En-Kesukquand -Nishnoh-Mohtompan-
(I pray to the Sun Spirit every morning.)
Nenawun-Tabuttantamoonk-Newutche-Kepenumoonk-Wunne-
(We give thanks for the good Harvest.)

Nenawun-Tabuttantamoonk-Newutche-Touohkomuk-Wunnegin-
(We give thanks for the beautiful forests.)
Nenawun-Tabuttantamoonk-Newutche —Wame-Metugquash-Kah-
Uppeshauanash-Wunnegin-Quinnupohke-
(We give thanks for all the beautiful trees and flowers
surrounding us.)
Nenawun-Tabuttantamoonk-Newutche-Nippissipogwash-Kah-
Pawtuckquash-Wunnegin-
(We give thanks for all the beautiful lakes and waterfalls.)
Nenawun- Tabuttantamoonk-Newutche-Nishnoh-Teag-Wunne-
(We give thanks for all good things.)
Taubotne- Manitoo- Nuttisowis - Neetskehheau- N'keke-
(Thank you, Creator. I am Healing Otter.)

He turned to all the people and said, "Something is about to
happen, that has never happened before. This is a day that has never
been. It is a day that we now share with one another. This is a New
Sun. With each new Sun is a new chance to grow. With each New
Sun is another chance to try a better way. To ask for forgiveness, or to
open our hearts, and forgive those who wronged us. With each New
Sun we have another chance to be in the light; to think clearly. We are
all blessed and we honor the Sun, for we are truly thankful that it did
not refuse to rise. The Sun, which is much older, wiser, and more
powerful than all of us, chooses to stay in harmony with Mother
Earth. Could we imagine a world where the Sun behaved as we do?"

Healing Otter took a brief pause, as he smiled and gazed to the
fire. "I want to tell you what my grandfather told me about the
'bravest coward' in the world. He told me, 'long ago, there was a very
fierce warrior, and he just loved to fight and show how brave he was.
He would go off in the woods and pick fights with the biggest

137

mountain lion, and then chase down the toughest pack of wolves, by his lonesome; he wouldn't leave them alone, until he made each one cry. After all of that, he wouldn't be done yet. He even wrestled down the angriest bears, in all of these parts. One early morning, as the fierce warrior was preparing his next hunt, he tripped over the pot in the Long House, spilling all the deer stew. That afternoon everyone went hungry. After much inquiry, nobody knew who knocked over the soup, except for one young girl, who was up early, and witnessed the incident. That evening the little girl said to the warrior, 'Why didn't you tell everyone it was you, who spilled the soup?' The embarrassed warrior put his head down in shame and said, 'I was afraid to admit I was wrong.' That story always reminds me of how brave that little girl was," he chuckled. Healing Otter looked around the circle and said, "Sometimes, my people, the hardest thing to do is to say we are wrong or we made a mistake, but just as the Sun has returned, so can hope, and another chance to grow. Have peace and love for all. That is why we light this fire, and keep it bright, for four days; it connects us to the entire universe, as well as the sun and all of its medicine." Healing Otter held his hand out towards the fire and said, "We light this fire in remembrance of all our Ancestors. The Sacred Fire opens up our path into the truth and will teach us. We share our thoughts, love, and good stories. My people, come up to the fire and share your words and open your heart."

People of all ages solemnly approached the Sacred Flame, sharing their words, stories, and hopes for the future. The steady beat of the drum seemed to affirm their prayers. Keenah gently made her way to the center and bowed her head. George walked up and joined her. Just as Silvia and Robert gathered with them, Healing Otter gave them both a soft pat on the head.

Neempau patiently waited his turn, then, with a troubled appearance, he knelt down next to the Sacred Fire. As the flames flickered before his searching eyes, he said in a low voice, "Mother, for you. Father, for you."

As he got up, he glared at the non-Native participants nearby. Neempau retreated near the Tribal drum group while he waited to speak to Healing Otter. The fire would now stay lit for four consecutive days with assigned Fire Keepers tending to it around the clock.

Now that the Opening Ceremony was just about completed, there would be a host of Tribal activities that would last throughout the Harvest Moon Ceremony: memorial services for past relatives and veterans, Water Drum singing and traditional dancing, storytelling from various Elders, Nipmuc language education, health information, and plenty of traditional foods, for those who are not fasting during this time. On the evening before the last day of Harvest Moon, there will be a Sweat Lodge Ceremony.

After Healing Otter shook hands and hugged everyone in attendance, he sought out Neempau and invited him for a walk. They strolled past the Longhouse and down a narrow trail that led to a creek, in the old growth forest. There was a clearing where a felled sycamore log served as a bench by the rushing brook.

The Elder put his arm on Neempau's shoulder and said, "So, I hear you and Martin have been spending some time together." Healing Otter puckered his worn but vibrant face. "Sure wish he was here; we have tried through the years, but as I say to you, Neempau, we must all find our way."

Neempau said, "Yes, Elder, I found my way, and that's to destroy Thanksgiving — to end it and expose it for all it is. Healing Otter, I mean no disrespect, but what are these non-Indians doing here? This is our ceremony, our teachings, not for the White man. Every time we get something, they got their nose in it trying to play as one of us. I've suffered all my life because of them; we all have. They don't belong here. I couldn't even pray right with these fakers around."

Healing Otter sat quietly with his head tilted, as if his slightly large ears were honing in on the intonation.

Neempau gazed into the tributary, as a few moments passed without a response from the Elder. Healing Otter then leaned forward a little and reached in his back pocket, took out a handkerchief and blew his nose. He then released a warm smile and said, "White people? Fakers? All I saw today were Human Beings. Yup. Yup. Neempau, my memory is still pretty good. When you were just a little thing, maybe six or seven years old, we would take you down to the river, and fish. That fishing spear was bigger than you. But you were strong, and after some time, you made a good, good catch. Your dad was so proud when you pulled up that fish. Heh. And we men —well, some of the other relatives were in a stiff competition on who could bring in the best catch, but your dad, he was sharp, and was always a good fisherman— and he always loved you."

Healing Otter continued on with the fish story as Neempau grew impatient.

Neempau was overcome with the urge to interrupt the Elder and said, "Elder, please, I'm talking about the White man trampling on our life and ceremonies."

Healing Otter replied, "Do you remember the ritual we do after we bring in the fish, Neempau?"

Neempau said, "Yes, of course. We put down an offering of Tobacco and ask for forgiveness."

"Why do we do that, Neempau?"

"We put down our Sacred Tobacco, because everything in creation has a spirit; we, we are connected to the fish."

Healing Otter nodded his head and said, "Mm, good, good. So you know the fish is our brother, as are the bear, crow, wolf, and turtle. This stream, the mountains, and the grandfather stones are all our relatives. Even the ant and hornets are our cousins. So, how is it, my son, that you believe that another Human Being is not part of you?"

Neempau's mouth fell open, his eyes heavy.

The Elder went on, "And not wanting to pray and share with another Human Being because they look different? Well, that's as far away from being an Indian as a blade of grass is from the Stars."

With a pained expression, Neempau uttered, "Well, come on. After all they've done. All their murdering and stealing? Now they wanna be part of our ceremonies?"

Healing Otter said, "I understand your words and can feel your troubled heart, but these ceremonies don't belong to us, Neempau. They are a gift from the Creator. We cannot control what we do not own. These ways were passed down to us and we are charged with the responsibility to share, as has been shared with us. The Sun does not pick and choose who to shine on; the wind does not blow in the opposite direction when approaching someone from another race."

The Elder rubbed his dry hands together, thoughtfully gazed up and said, "When I was just a little boy, there were signs that read 'No Indians Allowed.' I was spat on and called all kinds of horrible things. Some of our people were even killed and there was no law or justice to turn to. But, my son, you must understand the kind of people who would engage in these careless and reckless acts of hate, are beings with troubled hearts and minds. They act in opposition to nature, which sees all life as equal. They are sad with sick souls that have lost all connections with the living and only seek death. Hate only breeds hate, and poisons the heart."

"Then that's my point. Look how they are. Look how they treated you."

"No, No, my son, don't miss the point. As I told you, Manitoo came to our Ancestors long ago and taught us how to be in harmony with all life, to share, and to teach our young, and protect our old. Our ways don't change because some others have chosen an evil path."

"But haven't you seen it yourself? These Whites come in, exploit the culture, and make up crap, just like their stupid Thanksgiving."

"It is still the same my son. We cannot behave in an ill way because we fear others may do so, too. We cannot walk away or stop because some may choose to abuse what has freely been shared. If we do such things, then we cheat ourselves, and our culture, and then, become that which we wish to destroy."

Neempau winced with an expression of concern and tugged on his braids.

"Any Human Being who has walked the path of hate and bitterness only corrodes from the inside. I am much older than you and have seen many, many things; heard many stories from those who have passed long ago. I am very aware of the cruelty and wickedness that Human Beings can do to one another, but following them down that path will only make us become a reflection of the darkness we wish to defeat. Our medicine, like that stream down there, is alive, awake and always part of what we do. The Creator gifted us with this medicine; it came to our people, but it was meant to be shared. Every living thing that there is, is part of the Circle. We don't control it, Neempau. We, as Human Beings, only choose to be inside, or out." Healing Otter nodded his head, "But yes, yes, my son, we always need warriors, and our people have always had them, just like your parents. They fought to protect our right to pray and many other things. But I think you, my son, are fighting something else."

Neempau sprang up from the log and ambled over to a large tree, as if his legs were twice their weight. He leaned his head on the trunk of the oak, his eyes slightly moistened.

The Elder slowly got up and stood beside Neempau and said, "I want you to know that nobody ever blamed you for what happened. I know this to be true, Neempau. Sometimes, the fiercest and bravest warrior is willing to confront almost anything, but sometimes the biggest challenge is to confront ourselves."

Neempau struggled to hold back sniffles as Healing Otter patted his back.

Healing Otter then said, "Tell me, tell me – what is really in your heart?"

Neempau didn't answer but instead, awkwardly, turned his head side-to-side, as if searching for an object amongst the leaves and underbrush. He let out a strong, gusty breath, but remained silent.

Healing Otter calmly said, "It's alright. I am here to help in any way I can, as I told you. I've thought about you for some time; I have seen you in my dream, and what I saw was a man who has long troubled himself about things that are out of his control. But now, a new day has come. The Sacred Fire has been lit, the prayers offered, the Tobacco has been put down, the Pipe has been respected; everything that needed to be done has been done. Only thing left is for your heart to receive the medicine and the gifts that Creator has put before you."

Neempau closed his eyes for a moment and took a deep breath. He tapped on the tree and nodded with his head down.

"Okay— well, I'm getting a little tired," the Elder said, "I'm goin' home for a nap, but I will be back later this evening to offer prayers to the Fire. I hope to see you here tonight. I think it will help."

As the Elder began to make his way back up the narrow trail, he raised his creaky, worn voice and hollered, "Come back tonight, Neempau, and we will talk about Thanksgiving— and stuffing and all that."

Neempau turned in the direction of the Elder, with lost eyes, and watched him step away. As a tear rolled down his cheek, he gestured as if about to speak, but the words failed to come. A short time later, Neempau pulled himself together and rejoined the gathering. Robert and Silvia had joined in on some of the Water Drum social songs, while George and Keenah were socializing with other relatives.

After a couple hours passed, Keenah informed Neempau that she had to work in the evening. The family swapped hugs and said their farewells. Neempau paused for a long time by the Sacred Fire, and then walked to the car. As they drove away, Silvia and Robert were elated as they chatted about the ceremony. Keenah began telling George how she thought the hospital floor would be short on nurses that evening. Neempau sat quietly in the back entrenched in his own thoughts.

Chapter 10

Piuk

Once they arrived home, Neempau went directly to the guest room and closed the door. Within two seconds, Robert was knocking. "Uncle! Uncle!" Robert shouted.

"Hey, Robert. What's up?" Neempau asked as he cracked open the door.

Robert replied, "Uh, today was really cool, Uncle! I really like hearing our Nipmuc language. I was talking with Nantai. He's one of the kids that sings with the Quabbin Lake Singers, and he told me that if I wanna learn the language, to sign up with our cousin, Redvine. Nantai told me Redvine is the one who teaches the language. Boy, it will be nice to learn how to swear in Nipmuc."

Neempau raised his eyebrows and scowled just as the boy explained, "Oh, I was just joking around, Uncle; I wouldn't do that. But I wanted to ask you, are you still gonna come to the big football game? It's tomorrow."

Neempau replied, "Well, I'll see. You realize Harvest Moon Ceremony has just begun, right? I mean, hopefully you guys will go back, especially for the closing Circle."

Robert said, "Sure, Uncle Neempau. I figure the more I hear, the more I learn."

Neempau seemed to stare off in the distance. He then said, "Uh, yes, yes, the more we listen, the more we learn."

A spark lit within Neempau's soul and sent a bursting crackle of inspiration through his body. Suddenly, as every part of him felt lighter, he added, "Yes, Robert, we just have to know what we're searching for and what we're really fighting for."

With a puzzled look on his face, Robert said, "But, Uncle, I wasn't searching for anything. I think?"

Neempau replied, "It's okay, keep looking and it will come. We will talk later, okay? There's something I really need to do."

Neempau rushed downstairs and approached his sister. "Hey, Sis, what time are you leaving for work? Let me take you. I need the car. Please?"

Keenah said, "Whoa, whoa. Of course, but slow down; where's the fire?"

With a confident smile, Neempau said, "The fire is at our Reservation, and I need to go back."

With a faint grin, Keenah nodded. "Okay, I'll be ready shortly."

While Neempau waited, he took a moment to call Wavy's apartment. He wanted him to come along to the Sacred Fire with him. After 10 rings, he got no answer. Following several unsuccessful attempts, Neempau hung up the phone.

As Silvia walked in from the kitchen she asked, "Hey, Uncle, you're going back? I'll go with you. I wanna do some more of the old moccasin dances."

Neempau gently replied, "Well, maybe later, okay? There are just a few things I need to do. I'm sure proud of you guys."

Neempau glanced in the direction of the kitchen table, where George was sitting and reading the paper. George sat quietly, unaware that Neempau gave him a soft and thoughtful look. Neempau stepped forward as if he was about to tell George something. Before he could, Keenah called out by the front door, "Neempau! I'm ready!"

Neempau pulled back and went with his sister. Once they got underway, Neempau asked his sister, "Say, uh, Sis, are you still gonna have that Thanksgiving-dinner thing? Didn't you feel something today? Something big?"

Keenah replied, "Yes, of course, I did. I loved it. I can't remember the last time I went to a ceremony, like that. But I still don't see any reason not to have our dinner. Let me ask you this: why do I have to stop celebrating? I'm not honoring the 'White man,' as you say. This is about our family, nobody else. Geez, Neempau, after all these years of you being away, I just wish you could have come home on a more peaceful note."

Neempau sarcastically shouted, "Peaceful note?" He quickly took hold of himself then said calmly, "Peaceful note — you have no idea, Sis, none, at all. Look, I didn't mean to yell, there's just — well, Thanksgiving needs to end, then I'll be at peace."

There was very little conversation as they drove on. However, once Keenah arrived at the hospital, she shared some parting words to her brother, "Well, keep the car as long as you need it. I can get a ride home if need be. I hope you find what you're looking for. And you know what? I do know a few things, here, and there. Just gotta talk to me. Take care."

Neempau gave her an unhappy look as he drove away. He went over to Wavy's apartment and knocked on the door. Much like the earlier phone call, there was no answer. He knocked several times then started shouted out, "Hey, Wavy! Wavy, it's Neempau! You in there? Come on out, it's important! Come on, I want you to come to the Sacred Fire! Are you in there with a girl? Getting stoned? Wavy? Well, alright, I'm going—I need to—" Neempau shook his head and started walking away, "See ya later, Wavy."

Before he went any further, he was compelled to make a visit to the old cemetery where his mother and father were buried. After driving through the black iron gates, he parked the car along a secluded dirt road. He walked up the small hill by the weeping willow tree to their graveside.

Next to his parents' graves were several Nipmuc relatives of years past. Some of them having the insignia, "G.A.R. 1861-1865," etched on their stone. As the fall wind blew about his hair and ruffled his jacket, he went to his knees, and placed some Tobacco on the ground. He gently passed his hand over the carved stones, and softly uttered, "I'm sorry."

Neempau left the cemetery and made his way back to the Reservation, and drove to Allum Lake. With a small backpack, he walked around to the far side of the water, through thickets and trails, to a clearing by the shore. He climbed up on a large boulder, with a flat top that rested half in the water. He sat facing the West, as the day's Sun descended into its final hours.

He opened up his backpack and removed a bundle of Tobacco, sheet of red felt, and a small knife. He cut the felt into seven small squares. Next, he filled them with a pinch of Tobacco, and then tied them off, forming little red pouches. When he finished, he grasped all the red bundles in both hands and held them to his forehead.

Neempau stayed there and prayed to the fading Sun, as the mild waves splashed, and waded against the big stone.

As the evening set in, Neempau set off for the Sacred Fire, nearby. Upon his return, all was dark, except for the radiant, and inspiring Sacred Fire within his view. The bursts of glowing embers sparked, and danced, and invited Neempau to the Circle.

With stiff and nervous legs, he approached the Fire as if walking into the unknown. Then, as if appearing from the smoke, Healing

Otter was standing there holding the turtle shell rattle with an old familiar smile.

Neempau paused for a moment as he sadly gazed at the Medicine Man. The Elder's skin appeared to be a patina of shiny bronze and his dark eyes flickered to the harmony of the flame.

Healing Otter then gestured with his hand for Neempau to come forward. With watery and regretful eyes, Neempau slowly staggered onward as if he just completed a marathon. When he reached Healing Otter, he rested his head in his chest. The Elder patted his head and said, "Let us sit by the fire."

The Medicine Man shook the turtle shell rattle and said, "Tell me all that is in your heart, Son."

Neempau paused for a moment as the Sacred Light pulled him in. He began to feel light and faint. The harmonic sound of the rattle hummed and echoed within his soul. There were flashes of light, and faces, before his eyes. Suddenly, the flames swirled into a circle. The center of the blaze opened up like a passageway. It revealed Neempau's tormenting despair:

"They warned me about you. I've got a good notion to rip out all that heathen hair! You are not going to ruin this class's Thanksgiving Day activities with your nonsense. Now, you pick up that Indian hat you threw on the floor, or you'll spend the rest of the 4th grade in the corner, buster!"

As Neempau drifted into the depths of sad reflection, the Elder shouted, "Neempau! Don't just remember — let it all go! Give it to the fire."

Neempau wiped his face and took a deep breath. He placed the red bundles into the fire.

He slowly said, "It — it was a horrible time of my life. It changed everything, forever. That teacher."

Neempau began to open up and share what happened to him in his fourth-grade class. "I — I was in that closet all day. I even wet myself, but she wouldn't let me go home. All because I wouldn't dress up in the paper feathers. By that time, I was hungry, too, so when she made me go back to my seat, I thought I could at least eat. But she didn't let me; I sat there at my chair as they passed out cakes, candy, and cookies to all the kids but me. She made me sit there and watch them all eat. I was wet and hurt; so hurt, that I forgot that I was hungry. I felt embarrassed and ashamed."

As Neempau spoke, the Elder had his eyes closed and gently shook the rattle.

"This one kid who sat next to me tried to share, but the teacher would not let him. I can still see his uncomfortable look as he ate his snack. All I could think was, that it was me that was causing him pain. In a strange way, that hurt me too. Then my hurt turned to fear, then anger. The teacher said she was going to put me in the closet all week and she did, right up until Thanksgiving vacation. Each day I went home sadder than the last, but I didn't tell my parents, especially my dad. I don't have to tell you how he was; I knew he would do something. Not sure what, exactly, but I knew he'd do something."

Neempau paused, gazed into the fire, and then curiously looked around into the darkness, as if something were there.

"Anyway, it was my third day locked in that closet, and it was the day before Thanksgiving. By this time, my hurt and fear had turned me numb, and I hated this teacher so much. So this time when I got home, I told my dad what had happened to me all week. As the words landed on his ears, he fell to the floor in sadness and then surged up in a fit of rage. And that's when — that's when he stormed out of the house to deal with that teacher. He raced up to the school, but she had gone for the day. So, he went to talk with the school Principal and it turned ugly really fast."

Healing Otter placed some Tobacco and roots into the fire. He handed some to Neempau and gestured with his head for him to do the same.

The Elder said, "Keep speaking, my son. Let it all go."

"The Principal took the side of Ms. Nelson, which made my father even more furious. He began pounding on the desk demanding to speak to her. It got to the point where they called the police on him and kicked him off school property. But my father had never been one to give up on anything so easy. He looked up her address in the phone book and went to her house. He jumped out of his car and started banging on her door non-stop. Her husband came to the door with a look of shock; he had no idea who my father was. Plus, to see a big brown guy in that neighborhood also must have seemed odd to him. When my dad revealed who he was and what he wanted, the man slammed the door in his face."

Neempau took a deep breath as leaves shuffled in the darkness and the logs sputtered and hissed on the flame.

"Ms. Nelson was peeking down at my dad from behind a curtain of the upstairs window. He saw her and shouted, 'Get the hell out here! Explain to me what you have done to my son!' Dad started banging even harder on the door. Ms. Nelson's husband joined her in the window. He opened it a little and shouted back at my dad to go away. My dad didn't leave, though; he stayed there out on their front lawn yelling."

Neempau eyes reflected the glowing embers. He had his arms folded, as if he had the chills, and rocked back and forth.

"Then that's when it happened. About four or five cop cars pulled up to the house. They rushed out and started shouting for my dad to

151

get on the ground. He refused. He tried to tell them what the teacher had done, but they wouldn't listen. Suddenly, one of the officers hit him behind his neck with his club. Then another one hit him, then another, then another." Neempau paused, coughed and shook his head, "One of the last things my dad yelled was, 'Get your hands off me! I know my rights!' They began to hit him until he didn't move or talk. He was in the hospital for a month. The doctors said he was struck over fifteen times and was lucky to be alive, but my dad never walked again."

Neempau wiped the tears from his face.

"He was paralyzed from the waist down. I didn't understand it all, at that age, but as the years went by it began to sink in. My dad was in that wheelchair because of me. Because I opened my mouth." Neempau pressed his fists against his forehead, "And Keenah, my little sister," he said, "doesn't even know. She was too little at the time. Do you know what they told her? Dad got beat up by the cops at one of the rallies. Our lives changed so much after that. We still went to the gatherings and protests, but Dad wasn't the same. And that big van we had to get, plus Mom got sick; she had to do so much now. When my Dad died so young of complications from being in that damn chair, that was it for me. I knew it was my entire fault, and I couldn't stand to be here. I stayed away as much as possible."

"Yes, my son, tell me."

"I did the only thing I thought I could do at the time: sue the State for wrongful death. I wanted them to pay, but I lost the case. And appeal after appeal, it got denied. Last week, I received a letter telling me the appeals process had been exhausted. That's when I knew I had to do something. When Mom died of diabetes, I missed out on her too — I missed out on so much." Neempau picked up a rock on the ground, stood up and hurled it into the brush. He looked into the dark, sat back down and said, "I've just been so tired with myself and life, the only thing left for me to do was to keep their fight going: end Thanksgiving. It's been over 300 years and that holiday is still ruining the lives of our people. But now I just don't know anything anymore. I've been so full of rage all these years that all I want to do is keep the White world out. My father is gone and it's all because of me."

The Elder's gaze at Neempau was serious as he opened a small ancient buckskin pouch. He took out a pinch of herbs and placed them in the fire. This caused the flame to flicker, shake and reach for the Stars.

Healing Otter said, "Neempau, I have travelled many journeys with your father. We have shared many things, and this one thing I know, he never blamed you. In fact, he loved you and he did his duty as a father. He had no regrets. I know he wanted you to stop blaming yourself. As I have told you my son, the right actions cannot be compromised by the fear others may do wrong. White world? There is no White world, only this one world; the one world the Creator has made for all of his creatures to share. Just like these trees around us, the blowing wind, the four legged, and winged ones— What are you, Neempau?"

With a sad and confused look, Neempau replied, "I—I'm a Nipmuc Indian."

The Elder replied, "And what does that really mean to you? Absorb those words. Think on it."

While Neempau quietly watched the fire, Healing Otter said, "Nipmuc, the 'People of the Fresh Water', they call us, but it's really another word for 'Human Being.' We have always been on this land. The bones of our Ancestors are ingrained with the oldest of these mountains. These waters flow with the spirit of our people and the wind sings the songs of all our relations. The animals and birds follow us into our dreams and show us how to live. These are the lessons that go back to the beginning of all things. Yes, the Pilgrims came and dark and painful days followed with them. Oh my, they did their best to get rid of all the Indians, didn't they? Diseases, wars, taking our land. Then it was relocations, the Dawes Act, boarding schools, and on, and on, and on. All these things were done to take away who and what we are, but we are still here because of the foundation of our teachings. Our medicine is the way of the Earth, the Sun and all of Creation. We are still here because the ocean and Moon are still here. We are still here because the wind still blows. They cannot kill our spirits with bombs and guns, Neempau, or boarding schools, or forced relocations. By remaining who we are, what Creator has showed us, that is our true victory."

In a forlorn tone, Neempau replied, "But, it's hard. I—I've been trying to keep part of the world out for so long. Now, it feels as though I lost a piece of me with it. I mean, all that has gone wrong with Indians, especially with my father, and our Tribe — we still have so many problems that need to be resolved. I just want to help, to fight."

The Elder placed his hand over Neempau's heart and said, "It is right in here, son — this is where the battle begins. I know it is hard, but look — look at this Sacred Fire. It is our sacred, and eternal, medicine that connects us to the spirit world, and the universe. It also gives us warmth, lets us cook our foods, and gives us light, but when it is misused and not cared for properly, it becomes deadly to all in its path. So, I say to you, Neempau: keep telling the stories, be a warrior for the people – all people. The world will listen if you bring the light, but you do not have to burn the world. The truth always wins, son."

The Medicine Man put more herbs into the Sacred Fire as he shook the rattle and sang.

As Neempau sat reflecting on his life, the chant continued. Neempau's sight travelled deep into the Flame, and to the pulse of the ancient song. Once again, the Elder added a mix of dried leaves and roots to the flame. This time, though, the blend brought forth a whirling and twisting flash that shot out glowing balls of light. The orbs spun and danced around the Sacred Fire, through un-coiling white smoke. Then one of the bright spheres gently floated next to the round of cedar trees and hovered. As Neempau watched in awe, the radiance turned into a white mist that began to expand.

Then, as if materializing from the vapors, Neempau's father appeared between the trees, sitting in his wheelchair. As Neempau blinked and rubbed his eyes, his father gazed upon him with a peaceful and tranquil smile. Neempaus' father sturdily raised himself out of the wheelchair and walked to the fire. Neempau stared up at his father, through tear-drenched eyes, while trying to find the words to speak.

Healing Otter continued chanting and was focused on the flame.

Neempau's father looked at his son with a smile and said, "My boy, my son. I want you to be happy. Do not despair anymore. There is no need to hurt, there is no need to feel fault. I am always with you. I love you, son."

Suddenly, his father's presence waved and shimmered like the flame, then began to fade.

Neempau cried out, "Dad! Dad! W–Wait! Don't go!"

As the apparition disappeared, Neempau collapsed, in mournful tears, by the Sacred Flame.

Chapter 11

Nabo-Nequt

Neempau had lain by the fire all through the night. He was awakened at first light, thanks to a Downy woodpecker, who was working hard on a nearby oak tree. When he looked around, he noticed Healing Otter was not there. Nonetheless, the day felt brighter to Neempau.

Refreshed, he smiled and gazed up into the tall trees. He added a couple logs to the fire. Shortly after, Healing Otter reentered the Circle.

Neempau called out, "Hey, Healing Otter! Oh man, last night. My father. Did you see my—hey, where did you go last night? Did you go off to meditate?"

With a serious gaze, the Elder replied, "No, son, I went down to Billy Cornleaf's Breakfast Barn. I got me the mornin' special: bannock 'n eggs, with a nice cup of sassafras tea."

The Elder patted Neempau on the back as they both chuckled. Neempau then gave the Elder a sincere look, "Thank you; thank you for everything. But now what? What do I do?" he asked.

Healing Otter said, "Be the man you were always meant to be. Remember all the things you have learned; keep them close to your heart. It is a new day, my son; a new day."

At that moment, several other Tribal members joined in, tending to the Sacred Fire. Two of them had the duty of Fire Keeper as the ceremony continued into the second day.

After Neempau jubilantly greeted his relatives, he made preparations to depart for the day. He called out to the Elder and said, "Well, I guess I'll head out for now; I have some things I must take care of. I will be back tomorrow to take part in the activities, and then the Sweat Lodge Ceremony in the evening."

The Elder replied, "Good; that will be good. See if you can bring your cousin, Martin, with ya. One more thing, Neempau: get over to Billy Cornleaf's and try that bannock."

With a smile and nod, Neempau strolled away.

When he made it back to his sister's house, Robert was in the living room playing a video game. The boy jumped up when his uncle walked in and said, "All right, you're here! The big football game is this afternoon. You're coming, right? Right?"

Silvia, who was sitting in the kitchen with her boyfriend, yelled out, "Yeah, Uncle Neempau! Come with us; it will be fun!"

Neempau said, "Well, sure, sure, why not? Say, where are your folks?"

Silvia said, "They went out to do some last minute shopping for, umm–"

"Thanksgiving?" Neempau asked.

Silvia was uneasy and didn't wish to answer, but Neempau, sensing such, changed the subject. "Hey, uh, never mind. So, who's playing today?"

Silvia replied, "It's my high school against the Regional Champs from North Central; they're not as tough as us Lacrosse players," she chuckled, "but still fun to watch."

Shortly thereafter, Keenah and George arrived with grocery bags in their hands.

George called out, "Rob, Silvia! Go grab those bags from the car!"

As the kids went out, Silvia's boyfriend, Fredrick, went with them. Once they brought in all the groceries, Robert said, "Hey, Mom, don't forget that we gotta leave soon!"

While waiting to go, the three youths tossed a football in the backyard. Neempau quietly observed George and Keenah putting away the stuffing, yams, pies, assorted fruits, and canned goods.

With a mild voice, Neempau said, "Hey, uh, George, can we talk?"

Keenah made a slight grin and said, "You guys excuse me; I need to do something upstairs."

As his sister walked away Neempau said, "Say, George, I just need to tell you—well, I'm sorry about–"

"Hey," George abruptly cut in and, in an almost embarrassed fashion, said, "Hey, hey! No need to say anything."

Neempau said, "No, wait. There is a need. I haven't treated you right, or given you the respect that you deserve. You're a good father, raising a good family; a fine example for Nipmuc people."

As Neempau extended his hand he said, "And you are my brother."

George gave a relaxed sigh coupled with a beaming smile. The handshake turned into a brotherly hug.

Keenah returned to the kitchen. "Oh! Very nice! That would make such a great postcard," she said with a giggle. "This really makes my day to see my brother and husband getting along, that's what I'm talking about!"

Neempau took on a serious tone and said, "Well, Sis, speaking of talking, there's something I need to share with you—about what really happened to Dad."

George blurted in, "Well. Um, perhaps, I'll join the kids outside."

"No, George, it's alright," Neempau replied, "You can hear this, too. Sis, have a seat." Neempau tugged his braids a little, "I know you were told Dad was beat up at one of the protests, but he wasn't. You see, it was that fourth-grade teacher; she was putting me through hell. I told Dad and–"

Keenah stopped him. "Say no more. Mom told me what really happened a long time ago. I know this had nothing to do with anything you did. It's not your fault that someone hurt you. You were just a little boy." Keenah's eyes began to water as she went on, "Neempau, Dad was proud to stand up for his son. And maybe I didn't have the protesting spirit like the rest of the family, but what I did learn from all that is to stand up the best way I can. I mean, why do you think I went into nursing? With Dad disabled, then Mom coming down with diabetes, all I wanted to do was help people. And the one person I always wanted to help, was you."

Neempau eyes watered as he said, "And I was–"

"I know, Neempau. I know about the appeal denial. What matters now, is what we still have, and the beautiful memories they gave us."

The siblings embraced in a hug just as the kids came inside.

Silvia said, "Aaaw, so sweet! That would make a great postcard."

"Okay, everyone, let's go, I wanna get a good spot!" Robert said.

The family, along with Silvia's boyfriend, packed the minivan and set off, for the away football game. They arrived 30 minutes later at the field, with hundreds of other rambunctious fans who have come out to support their team. They were able to get a section near the front and center field, on the quickly filling bleachers. The cheerleaders rapidly entered the arena as they awaited the start of the game. At the edge of the wooden green benches, there was a connecting tower made of brick and wood, where the announcer was seated.

He gave the cheerleaders a rip-roaring welcome over the, slightly crackling, loudspeakers. The girls performed stunts and flips, which dazzled the crowd. The marching band brought the audience to a robust applause as they also took front and center. The stadium was completely filled. Neempau's attention was caught by the following announcement: "Happy Thanksgiving, ladies and gentlemen, and thank you for coming out to the pre-Thanksgiving Pumpkin Bowl Championship! We welcome the South County Titans and, our home team and returning Champions, the North Central Indians!"

The crowd went into a raucous ovation; and the high school band began to play the North Central theme song. It was an old fashioned so-called "Indian drum song." The lyrics and tempo were reminiscent of a 1930s or 40s Hollywood Western, much like Ethel Merman's "I'm An Indian, Too."

Neempau puckered his face and smiled as he gazed around the bleachers and took notice how the crowd was enjoying the performance. An uncomfortable heaviness came over Keenah, George and the kids as the band played on.

Fredrick shook his head and said, "Wow, that's messed up."

Silvia said, "Tell me about it. I thought they were gonna stop doing this."

Robert said to his uncle, "Hey, we don't sound like that."

Neempau paused and thought about how he would respond to the situation and said, "Nope. You're right, Robert, we don't sound like that. But you know what, I really feel sad for all these people who don't know the beautiful sound of our Water Drum."

Keenah projected a rosy, and pleased, smile at her brother. As the rest of the crowd cheered, the Nipmuc family let off a collective sigh of relief as the cheesy 'Tribal score' ended. After a short while, things seemed to have smoothed out as a very action-packed, and competitive, football game was underway.

But once again, Neempau's new-found serenity would be put to the test. About three rows up and to the left, a large, rowdy group was really getting into the game. One lady continually screamed out "Go, Indians! Go!" Next she added the infamous, all-purpose, generic "Indian war cry" "Whoop-Whoop-Whoop!" and on and on she went. After 15 minutes of sporadic 'war cries,' Neempau had heard enough.

He got up from his seat and maneuvered his way up to the lady. Neempau calmly sat down next to her as she continued to do her whooping. The woman greeted him with a smile as she stared at his long braids. He put out his hand and said, "Hello, my name is Neempau Stoneturtle."

The lady said, "Oh hello! I'm Samantha Rojeski."

Neempau replied, "See those people down there? That's my family, and we're all Nipmuc Indians. Those kids down there have a lot of pride in who they are, and they brought me here to watch their team play, and have a good time. Now, they're pretty uncomfortable by that thing that you're doing. It's very offensive, and sends a bad message to these kids who just want to enjoy the game."

The lady's eyes opened wide and she replied, "Oh my, I'm so sorry, I–"

Neempau cut in and said, "No, but please. I'm not here to interfere with you enjoying the game, and I can't tell you what to do, but I just wanted you to be aware that making that noise is offensive and stereotypical. It makes a mockery of who we really are."

Samantha said, "Oh my, my, thank you for telling me; I had no idea. I won't do it, again."

Just behind her, a man took issue with the compromise.

The man said, "What? You kiddin' me? I'll do it; I'll make that noise all day long. When I was a kid, my parents took me to this field and we always did the official war cry! It's just a game; get over it already."

The man demonstrated his freedom of speech by obnoxiously and loudly doing the war cry. For added effect, he also rapidly patted his mouth. Then he got within inches of Neempau's face, as he whooped and howled. Neempau became furious and clenched his fist, but just at the same moment, Keenah grabbed him. "Don't worry, I got this, Big Brother!"

Keenah stepped in front of her brother. "You know what? You sound like a complete idiot, and if you mess with my brother, you mess with me!"

George also made his way up there, stepping in front of Keenah and said "And that's my brother-in-law and my wife! Before you say anything to either of them, you deal with me!"

The lady stood up and said, "Yeah! And I'm Samantha Rojeski. Why don't you just leave this game if you can't respect others? So what if you've been doing that since you were a kid? Can't you see it's offensive?"

The man was nervous and overwhelmed, but tried to maintain his ground as a back and forth argument ensued. But this all abruptly ended when there was a sudden shriek from the lower right side of the seating.

"Snoods! My snoods!"

It was Mr. Mondo Snood, himself, who had come out to the game, and what he was frantic about was the madcap chaos that was underway below.

Throughout the stadium, jaws dropped and heads jolted in utter shock. Hundreds, upon hundreds of turkeys had taken to the field and flocked around in a crazed frenzy.

The football field sat at the edge of the forest wood line, and the turkeys made their way on the turf from a small trail behind the end zone. The stunned players darted around the field in a confused hysteria. Some of them ran for the locker rooms, through a storm of loose feathers, as the overwhelming force of the flapping gobblers seized the 50-yard line. Spectators hastily cleared out of the bleachers. Some of the players, adults, and Mondo Snood attempted to round up the birds.

One turkey became very angry and decided it wasn't going to run. The player who was in hot pursuit of the bird was also still carrying the football. The enraged bird let off a loud squawk, flapped its wings and rushed at the boy. Startled, the youth ran, shaking and baking, down the field. He tightly held the football as the large bird gave chase. The turkey matched his maneuvers and nipped at the back of his cleats. One quick-thinking coach observed the threat. He leapt for the fowl, but overshot his target and drove himself into the grass. The turkey, undeterred, kept up the attack until the player tripped near the end zone. He fell prone and fumbled the football. The turkey, joined by two others, leapt over him, as they scampered back into the woods.

Neempau painfully looked on, in an embarrassing grin, as a swarm of spectators zipped past him.

The announcer said over the loudspeaker, "Please, please, everyone remain calm! We'll clear the field and get back to the game. Oh, oh my gosh! Those snoods are huge!"

He awkwardly cleared his throat. "Um, oh, excuse me!"

The fans retreated across the road or to their cars, until the fowl play was restrained.

A large portion of the birds were captured, but more than half made a successful escape.

Following an hour of chasing birds and cleaning droppings, the game resumed.

Despite the earlier incidents, Neempau and his family were able to enjoy the rest of the game. Especially, since Silvia's high school won with a score of 42 to 36.

The family laughed and joked, all the way home, about the day's debacle, and Robert took some feathers home too. Once they returned to the house, Neempau said, "Okay, everybody, I'm gonna cook tonight. Show you guys a taste of the Nord," he laughed, "I learned this dish when I was up near René –Levasseur Island."

Keenah smiled and said, "Nice. Well, you're sure in a good mood; does this mean you're gonna have Thanksgiving with us?"

Neempau smiled back and said, "Now Sis, let's not get too carried away."

A few minutes later, the phone rang and Keenah went to answer. "Hello? — What?" Keenah screamed, "Oh my God! No!"

George ran over to her. "What? What is it?" he asked.

Keenah said, "It's Wavy! He's at my hospital in the intensive care unit! He tried to kill himself!"

Neempau jolted and dropped the mixing bowl on the floor.

Chapter 12

Nabo-Neese

Neempau seized his sister's car keys and sped to the hospital. After barreling through the ER doors, he raced to the main desk and said to the receptionist, "Wavy! I'm here to see Wavy. Tell me the room!"

The nurse did a quick check on the computer. "Sir, we have no patient here by that name."

Neempau uttered, "I—I mean Martin! Martin Attuck, Jr.! Where is he? Can you tell me his room?"

She gave him a sharp glare and turned back to her computer. She then replied, "Sir, that patient is in the intensive care wing, in room 372."

Just as the lady gave him the number, he tore for the elevator. He got up to the floor, and then ran at full speed down the corridor. As he approached the door, he began to move in slow motion. Instead of immediately entering, he sadly peered at his comatose cousin from the small glass window. Sitting at his bedside was his ex-wife Naomi and his two children.

Wavy had swallowed a large amount of opiates earlier that morning. Shortly afterward, he was feeling extremely dizzy and weak. Realizing he was in trouble, and perhaps regretful, he managed to stumble to his front door. He collapsed and landed on his head. A neighbor spotted him as he was lying face down, bleeding, and twitching on his front steps.

Blood was gushing from his mouth and nose. His fingernails and lips were quickly turning blue. His breathing was faint. Once the ambulance arrived, the driver quickly cut off Wavy's bloody clothes from his body. At the same time, another medic rapidly went to work on him, as they rushed him off to the hospital.

When they reached the emergency room, the doctors swiftly gave him several doses of Narcan, and performed other life-saving measures. They were able to stabilize his condition, but they had to transfer him to the intensive care unit, because he was still unresponsive.

At this point, he was hooked up to an IV and a heart monitor; he also had a breathing tube protruding from his mouth. There were five sutures put in on the side of his chin. Under both his eyes, he had bruising and his lips were cut and chaffed.

Neempau looked on in horror for several moments. He partially opened the door. Just as he did, Naomi, and her weeping children, had risen from their chairs and were preparing to leave. She paused for a moment, and gave Neempau a dejected stare, as she exited the room. Neempau looked back but quickly dropped his head.

He turned his attention to his cousin. His eyes gradually scanned up and down, while his mouth hung open. He then made a distressing sound, wincing at the sight of his cousin. After he cleared his throat, he uttered in a low voice, "Ooh, Wavy. Why?"

He stopped speaking and became dazed, but then he gently held Wavy's hand and whispered, "Hey, Cuz. It's Neempau. Can you hear me? I'm here, man. Aw, Wavy. Why didn't you talk with me?"

Neempau momentarily looked to the white floor and said, "I— I'm so, so, sorry, man. I should have seen it. I should have seen it. Oh, Wavy. I wish you would have just come to the fire. So much has happened; so much, thanks to— thanks to your dad. I know there's much work to do, but we don't have to keep suffering, Wavy, we don't. Because, you see, I was heading the same way. I didn't wanna live thinkin' I caused my family pain. But now— I know I didn't. I didn't, Wavy. I was wrong. Wrong, all these years—huh, wrong about a lot of things."

Neempau grabbed some tissue to dry his eyes. A nurse walked in to check on the IV bag.

She said to Neempau, "Can I get you a drink?"

"No–no, thank you."

Neempau eyes shifted from the intravenous bag, the nurse and then to Wavy.

The nurse smiled at Neempau as she left the room. Neempau nodded.

Neempau walked over to the window and looked out. He pulled at his braids, and looked up as if he were counting, and took a deep breath.

He walked back over to the bed, his hand running alongside the bedpost as he sat down.

"When I got the final appeal denial, I wanted to die. Suing the State was to be my revenge for everything, so what did I have left when that was over? I can spend my whole life hating that teacher who hurt me, and those cops who hurt my dad, but in the end, that hate eats us up from the inside. I don't think I came to this world just to hate. That's not what my mom and dad taught me; they taught me the message of hope, not the message of hate."

The beeping sound of the heart monitor resonated throughout the room.

Over the intercom, "Dr. Greer, please report to wing four nurses' station."

"My dad has passed, but I think he sent your dad to save my life. Not just to live, but to really see the world and the beauty– the beauty of what Creator made us. This whole Thanksgiving thing? Huh, I've hated that day for so long that I missed the more important point. The point is that we survived. Yeah, Cuz – you, me and the millions of Indians, across this country are still here. And we've done more than just survive. We have a voice; a voice to tell our story, not just to burn people up, but be bright enough to shine on them, something they need to see, Wavy."

Neempau took a tissue and gently patted the side of Wavy's mouth.

With a nervous chuckle, Neempau said, "You're gonna be okay, Wavy. You're my cousin and best friend. It's funny, you say you don't wanna be like your dad, but in many ways you are already walking in his beauty. You never judge anyone, you just try to love all people," With a faint smile he added, "Maybe, sometimes a little too much."

"You have a beautiful family man, they love you. You got a—"

Neempau swallowed, looked to the door, and then stared at the heart monitor to focus his words. "I never told this to anyone, but I've been afraid almost all my life. I never wanted to come back home. By staying away, I missed out on my niece and nephew, my sister, and even getting the chance to really know her husband. So, I came back home, believing I needed to do something big to feel whole—to free my soul. But the truth is, Wavy, I came back to free my heart. You can't die. You can't die on me. You are a special and talented person. Any movie producer should be honored to have you in their film."

Neempau reminisced over old stories through the night. After growing weary of talking over several hours, he rested his head at the side of his cousin's bed and fell asleep.

Around 11:00 A.M. Wednesday morning, Neempau awoke from his sleep in the uncomfortable chair. When he looked over at Wavy, he saw that the breathing apparatus had been removed from his mouth. Neempau quietly got up from his chair and walked out to the nurse's station down the hall. He asked the nurse, "Uh, excuse me. Martin Attuck: how is he? Is he gonna be alright?"

The nurse called to the doctor in the next room. The doctor walked over, looked at the clipboard and said; "I see on his chart that you're a relative so I can tell you. Looks like he's going to recover. We're going to re-check his labs, but it looks like he will be able to go home tomorrow. He just needs plenty of rest."

Neempau gave a slight nod and closed his eyes in relief. As Neempau was walking back towards the room, the nurse shouted, "Go tell your cousin he'll be home, just in time, for Thanksgiving."

Neempau froze in his steps, and with a tight smile, said, "Uh, yeah. Yeah, thank you."

Back at the Reservation, the third day of Harvest Moon Ceremony was underway. Today was the traditional Giveaway. This is where all the different Nipmuc families come and bring items to share with those in need, whether it is food, a bicycle for a child, wampum or leather for regalia, or just about anything they wished to share. All the Giveaway items would be brought to the Longhouse and placed in the middle of the lodge. Whatever the item that was needed, a person would simply take it and then place a small bundle of Tobacco down as a thank you. After all the gifts were dispersed, all the bundles of Tobacco would be picked up and offered to the Sacred Fire.

This event was followed by a grand Harvest Moon Feast. On the menu was venison chili, smoked salmon, baked pheasant, and moose pie. Other dishes included; a large pot of fresh roasted corn on the cob – roasted in their own leaves, succotash, corn soup, wild rice, sweet

171

potato pudding with walnuts, and tons of fresh bannock bread. After that, the people danced and sang on the Water Drum, all through the evening.

Before Wavy's hospitalization, Neempau had planned on being part of the day's events, but instead remained at the hospital.

Wavy slowly began to move about in the bed. He then partially opened his eyes and said in a groggy, and scratchy tone, "Hey, Cuz."

Neempau jumped up from the chair and said, "Aw man, Wavy, how do you feel?"

In a hoarse voice, Wavy said, "Like crap."

Neempau replied, "Look, um, there's a lot of things I wanted to share with you but, I guess you didn't hear me."

Wavy replied, "Cuz, I heard ya. It was a like a dream, but I heard ya. I just wanted to tell you one thing."

Neempau leaned in and asked, "What, Wavy?"

"Stay gold."

Neempau said, "Stay– stay gold?"

Wavy uttered, "Uh, ya—Johnny to Ponyboy – The Outsiders? "

Neempau hesitated for a moment, as he tried to recall the film. He laughed, and then said, "Aw, Wavy, yeah. Yeah, okay. I've seen that movie, but in this story, 'Johnny' lives; he lives, Wavy."

Wavy slowly closed his eyes for a moment. A lone tear rolled onto the blankets as he whispered, "Yeah, Cuz. He lives. He's gonna live— Cuz, get me some water."

As Neempau poured the drink, Wavy said in a regretful tone, "Oh, I don't know what I was thinkin'. I just felt I had lived enough, seen enough failure. So, I swallowed those pills, but then, like a light, I seen the faces of my boys and I knew I couldn't leave yet."

Neempau hugged his cousin and said, "We're gonna be alright, Wavy."

As the day came and went, Neempau stayed by Wavy's side as he recovered his strength. In the evening, Neempau told his cousin, "Listen, Wavy, I'm gonna be heading out for a while. Tonight is the Sweat Lodge Ceremony. I'm going in to say some prayers for you, for my parents, for everything."

Wavy groaned and began to rise and said, "Ok, Cuz. I'll go with you."

"No. Out of the question. Your body is way too weak right now for that. You know how it is Wavy; a Sweat Ceremony is a big deal, takes a lot out of the body. When our people have a Sweat Ceremony; the conditions, and the body, have to be correct. If not, people can get seriously hurt, even die. But hey, I'm glad you wanna go. Say, uh, the nurse told me your father was here last night while we both were sleeping."

"My father? I'm sure he's very pissed."

Neempau replied, "I doubt it, Wavy. I'm sure he's just happy you're alive. He loves you too. What I'm learning is that sometimes the hardest people to help, are the ones closest to us. When I came in last night, Naomi and your kids were here. I know you still love her. Just maybe there's still hope for you two. I don't know. But first, you gotta take care of yourself."

"Yeah, I know, I know, Cuz."

"Well, you're starting to look a lot better than last night. Call me if you need anything – anything. I'll see you soon."

Before he went to the ceremony, Neempau made a stop as his sister's home. As he walked up to the front door, George and Keenah were standing outside.

Keenah said, "I'm going up to see Wavy. I'll make sure he gets everything he needs."

Neempau smiled, and then asked George, "Okay, you ready?"

George replied, "This will be my first Sweat Ceremony, but I think so."

Neempau said, "Let's do this, Brother."

The men made their way to Harvest Moon just as the glowing red-hot Grandfather stones were ready to enter the lodge. There were several men present who were in the process of smudging, and praying, as they prepared to enter. Two of them were non-Native, one of who was Healing Otter's helper. The man shot an uncomfortable glance at Neempau.

Neempau approached him, paused for a moment but then extended his hand and said, "I don't think I properly introduced myself. I'm Neempau Stoneturtle, and thank you for sharing with us."

The gentleman brightened up and replied, "Thank you. Thank you for welcoming me into the Nipmuc Circle."

Neempau calmly said, "Hey, we're all just Human Beings. We are all part of the same Circle."

As George and Neempau smudged, a few other Nipmuc men began an old song. Soon thereafter, all the men entered the sacred darkness of the Sweat Lodge; returning to the womb of the mother for prayer, forgiveness, and guidance.

It was almost sunrise on the morning of both Thanksgiving and Harvest Moon when the Sweat Ceremony was complete. At about nine in the morning, Neempau and George returned home. When they arrived, Keenah and Silvia were up early preparing for the big Thanksgiving dinner. The sweet aroma of maple-drizzled roasted turkey and corn bread stuffing, baking in the oven, caressed every corner of the home. A trio of buttered yams, squash, and corn, with a large slice of bacon fat simmered on the stove. Next to it was a pot of wild rice, with added blueberries and strawberries. Warming on the other burner was garlic and rosemary mashed potatoes, with a side of gravy. Across from that, was a steaming kettle of green beans with lemon and pine nuts.

The caramel pumpkin, apple, and cranberry cobbler pies cooled on the black soapstone countertop, next to the coffee maker. George looked around and said, "Whoa— my girls did it again! Hey, the Sweat Ceremony was amazing! I'm not gonna say too much about that, though; that stays in the Lodge" he added with a sense of familiarity. "I will say this, though – I'm starving. I'm sure your brother is, too! Isn't that right, Neempau? Well, let me go change upstairs. I'll be down in a bit."

Before George went upstairs, he made a surreptitious detour that took him near the pies. He attempted to break off a piece, but failed due to the light slap on his hand from his wife.

With an uncomfortable smile, Neempau observed the festive scene. Neempau commented in a low tone, "So, this is it. Thanksgiving."

Keenah walked over to her brother and gave him a hug and said, "I hear Wavy is doing better."

Neempau replied, "Yea, he's gonna be alright. He's gonna get the help he needs. I have to– well, uh, the Closing Circle is at dusk, and that will conclude the Harvest Moon Ceremony. So–"

"Hey wait!" said Keenah. "I think we all should go to the Closing Circle, so why don't we go together after we have dinner?"

Silvia shouted, "Yeah! Please stay for dinner; Fredrick and his family will be coming over, too."

Neempau smiled, gave a subtle nod, and said "Well, I –some of the Tribal members and I are gonna drive up to Plymouth to take part in the Day of Mourning, but we'll be back in time for the closing Circle."

Keenah said, "I understand." She then raised her eyebrows and added, "Um, some of the Tribal members, huh? I think I heard Harriet is going, too."

Neempau blushed, "Uh, yeah, yeah, she is." Changing his tone to a serious one he said, "Today will be a day to teach and to share as our Ancestors did. We will mourn those who were lost and remember their sacrifice."

Abruptly, there was the honk of a horn in the driveway. It was Harriet.

Neempau hugged his sister and said, "Okay, I better get going, I'll see you guys tonight, at the Closing Circle."

As Neempau walked out the door and down the brick path, his attention was drawn to the home two houses down. A girl who looked about nine years old with golden blonde pigtails, was running out to a car. She was greeting her grandparents who had just pulled up. The old man embraced the child with a hug as he spun her around. Then the grandmother leaned in and kissed her on the cheek. As the elderly man put her down, the girl quickly grabbed him by the hand, leading him into the house.

Instead of getting in the car with Harriet, Neempau was drawn towards that residence. He slowly walked near the home as if engrossed in deep reflection. When he reached the house, the large picture window in the front gave him a clear view inside.

He observed several people – some sitting and others standing – by a finely-set Thanksgiving spread. A few were laughing, as one gentleman in a gray polo sweater appeared to be reciting a story.

The others cheered on the man in the Polo sweater as he, humorously, waved his hands high above his head. He abruptly covered his eyes as a woman, maybe his wife, rubbed him on his head in a playful manner.

Neempau then watched as the elderly couple that had just arrived, were receiving hugs and kisses from all those present. Neempau intensely looked on with a timid smile.

Abruptly, he was tapped on the back of the shoulder and Harriet softly said, "Is everything alright?"

Neempau gently turned to her and took pause. He then fashioned a big smile and replied, "Yes, it was always all right. Let's go."

Harriet and Neempau arrived at Plymouth just as the Day of Mourning Ceremony began near Coles Hill. After the opening prayers and acknowledgements, several Tribal leaders went up to a podium and shared words of the struggle and successes of their nations, before the hundreds who have gathered. Some leaders delivered fiery, and compelling, words that spoke of the travesty and injustices that Native Americans have suffered. Others talked about the spiritual unity of everyone, and the importance of all Humankind to come together to save our Mother Earth.

Then it was Neempau's turn to share some words before the masses. Harriet kissed him on the cheek and said, "I know you're gonna do great."

Neempau shyly smiled then walked to the platform. He looked down for a moment and closed his eyes. He lifted his head, adjusted the microphone and gazed across the crowd. "To all of my Ancestors, and to all the Elders and leaders here today, I'm honored to share this time with you. And we honor and respect this ancient Wampanoag land we stand on. To all of you who have come out on this day, I thank you. My name is Neempau Stoneturtle, member of the Turtle Clan of the Nipmuc Tribe. I stand on the shoulders of my mother and father, who lived their life fighting for the rights of Indigenous people, and many times just fighting for our right to exist. They are no longer with us but I just wanna say: Mom, Dad, I love you and thank you. Because of them, I am here today."

A few of the spectators shouted out, "Aho!" Neempau made a slight smile and continued on. "My life was not easy. I suffered because of the ignorance of others not understanding who we are, as I'm sure many of you here know what I mean. Then I had to see my father suffer from that same ignorance, and it was more than I could bear, so I spent most of my life staying away from my own land, and hating the White man. Recently I came home to end their Thanksgiving where it all started, but as I made this journey home, I began to realize some things as I listened to the words of my Elder, Healing Otter. All these years of anger and hate, has cheated my own spirit. We don't need to end their Thanksgiving." Neempau paused as he looked out to the ocean. "What I remember most about being an Indian kid, is all of the family and love around the home; Relatives just getting together, with a drum and potluck meal, and we were happy. I think that to most of Americans, Thanksgiving is just that; family and people just coming together to share good times, to share love. Why would anyone want to stop that? But what we do want to stop is the ignorance and injustice. So, I say this to you, the United States of America. You said you're a nation of laws? Then we say, stop breaking your own laws when it comes to Native Americans! You still have a lot to answer to!" The crowd erupted into a loud applause and shouts of, "Yeah!" Neempau nodded his head, and his body seemed energized by the affirmation of the people. His voice, slightly louder, and more determined as he went on, "My Nipmuc people, my Indigenous brothers and sisters across the world, have been denied their inherent rights for too long. We still have much work to do. Massasoit dreamed big! He dreamed of a unity that could happen, that was meant to happen. On this huge and abundant continent, my Ancestors gladly shared what they had with the new arrivals. Now, Indians everywhere are swept to the side in the far corners of society, and mostly only being mentioned around this time of year, or as a sports team mascot. You know, our Ancestors were right to share; it is our traditional way. And I believe, in most people's hearts, Indian or not, is a mind to share. I was once told, 'we should never stop doing the right thing just because we think others may do wrong.' So after all your turkey is gone, and the football game has ended, and you've eaten the pumpkin pie, and had your eggnog, think of us and learn the truth, but not with the fake images and stereotypes. Think of us and see us – see us as we are, because we're gonna be right here. We have always been here, but you just have to listen to us to get the truth. Thank you for listening."

Harriet nodded with a smile, as Neempau received a vigorous applause. The two of them walked through the crowd, greeting, and hugging folks from various Tribes. They ended up standing in front of Plymouth Rock. A young White police officer approached Neempau. He was one of the officers assigned to monitor the gathering. In a humble voice, he said to Neempau, "Thank you, I learned a lot today." The officer smiled and extended his hand. Neempau replied, "Thank you." And the two men shook hands.

A short time later, Harriet and Neempau departed Wampanoag land and returned to the Nipmuc Reservation to make it in time for the Harvest Moon Closing Circle. As they arrived, many Nipmucs along with dozens of non-Natives were forming a large circle around the Sacred Fire. Neempau walked around and greeted each person with a hug, and a handshake, as Harriet did the same. Keenah, George, Silvia, Robert, and Fredrick joined the circle around the fire. The Frogman was also there. He had on a worn-down corduroy jacket and his old military cap with an eagle feather on it.

He limped over to Neempau and said, "I made this especially for you." It was a dreamcatcher. As he handed it to him, he added, "Sleep well, my boy."

Neempau nodded. "Thank you." Then he gave the Frogman a hug.

Healing Otter was walking towards the gathering. By his side was his son, Wavy, who gingerly walked with him. Beside Wavy, were Naomi and their two boys.

Neempau beamed with joy as his eyes gazed around the Sacred Circle. Keenah beheld the Fire with moist eyes full of rejoice. With a thoughtful smile, George proudly, and earnestly listened to the closing prayers delivered by Healing Otter.

Robert heeded and absorbed the moment like a sponge. Silvia slightly nodded her head, and closed her eyes as she allowed the Spirit of the Ceremony to connect her to the Old Ways. Fredrick relaxed his shoulders as he comfortably, and respectfully, took part in the Nipmuc tradition.

As Wavy held up the smudge bowl, his father fanned the Eagle Feather one last time as the Sacred Fire Ceremony concluded.

After the embers cooled, each person gathered a small amount of ash from the fire to put in a bundle or pouch. The Sacred Ash would be carried as spiritual medicine, or passed on to a relative, or friend in need of healing. As the auburn Sun began to bend away, everyone began exchanging hugs, packing, and saying their farewells. Amidst the several dozen people heading home and moving about the Reservation, Neempau saw Wavy by the Longhouse.

The two men made eye contact across the way and shared a reflective moment of triumph. Naomi put her arm around Wavy and the two walked toward Healing Otter's pickup truck.

Neempau smiled, and chuckled under his breath, as he walked out with his sister and family. Just as Neempau was about to get in

Keenah's car, Harriet pulled beside him and asked, "Say, can I give you a ride to her house?"

Neempau jokingly replied, "Geez, I just love Nipmuc people; they always wanna give me a ride."

When Neempau arrived at his sister's home, he was surprised to see the entire Thanksgiving dinner was yet to be eaten. Neempau asked, "Sis? What's going on? Your dinner?"

Keenah replied, "Remember big Bro, every day is Thanksgiving, so we don't need any special time, or day. Now, eat with us."

Robert shouted, "Yes! Please, I'm starving. All Mom let me eat was peanuts!"

Harriet smiled at Neempau, as he declared, "Okay, but there's one thing we need to do before we eat."

Neempau, with the assistance of George, Silvia and Robert, prepared a scrumptious plate with a little bit of everything on it. Next, they took the plate outside and set it by a large oak tree in the backyard. George placed Tobacco all around the plate and said a prayer. They returned to the house.

Neempau turned to his nephew. "Robert, I want you to have this." Neempau removed his beautiful wampum necklace and gave it to the boy. He then gifted his niece a gorgeous beaded bracelet he got from Wampanoag land.

Back on the Nipmuc Reservation, the clear night sky fluttered with an array of colorful and joyful bursts, from its highest point. After Wavy lit off three more Roman candles, he sat down closely beside Naomi and their children.

Fredrick's parents, Harriet, and the whole family assembled around the large table and began their feast. As the potatoes and gravy were passed, Robert shouted, "Uncle Neempau, tell us a story!"

Neempau put down the fork and turned to Keenah and said, "Hey Sis. Remember the story 'Gift of the Strawberry' we heard growing up?"

As she sliced her turkey, she replied, "Ooh, yeah. Let's hear it."

Harriet added, "Yeah, I love that one."

The family gently moved about forks and plates, as they focused on the coming tale. Neempau gazed around the table. He then began with, "Ladies and gentlemen, this is one of our ancient stories; the 'Gift of the Strawberry.' Long ago, there were two Nipmuc siblings; a little boy and his, slightly, older sister. The siblings would always argue over silly things. After being tired of arguing so often, the sister was so upset she decided to run off deep in the woods. Now, when that happened she…"

The End

About the Author

Larry Spotted Crow Mann is an internationally acclaimed writer/poet, performer, Nipmuc cultural educator, Story Teller and Citizen of the Nipmuc Tribe. He serves as the Drum Keeper of the Tribe which is a Sacred trust. He travels throughout the United States, Canada and parts of Europe to schools, colleges, Pow Wows, and other organizations sharing the music, culture, and history of Nipmuc people. He has also given lectures at universities throughout New England on issues ranging from Native American sovereignty, to identity.

In 2010, his poetry was a winner in the Memescapes Journal of Fine Arts, and in 2013, his poetry was nominated for the Pushcart Prize.

Mann's previous book, Tales From the Whispering Basket is internationally acclaimed and has received excellent reviews.

Among his other important work, Mann has worked in collaboration with the Massachusetts Department of Public Health in creating the booklet "Coming Home: A Guide to Help in the Prevention and Treatment of Substance Abuse of Native American Youth".

Mann also contributed to the book, by Kathleen Noyes, Ed.D., "Stories of Educational Journeys: Indigenous - Learning & Socio-Cultural Approach in Education."

Mann was applauded for his role in the PBS Native American film, "We Shall Remain," directed by Chris Eyre.

Mann was also featured in two documentaries- Winner of the NPS 2007 Award for Interpretive Media "Living in Two Worlds: Native American Experiences on the Boston Harbor Islands," and "First Patriots," produced by Aaron Cadieux.

Furthermore, Mann has worked in the field of Human Services for over 12 years, mostly in the field of Mental Health and helping at risk youth.

* Publishing's include the "Memescapes Journal of Fine Arts" at Quinsigamond College.
* Indian Country Today Magazine
* Contributing work in the book, by Margaret Barton, "New England on Fire"
* Dawn Land Voices "Native American Anthology of New England," University of Nebraska Press

His poetry and quotes have been included in:
* Go Green Conference for the Medical Services Administration of Puerto Rico
* WordCraft Circle of Native American Writers
* "My Heart Is Red Project: A Journey Across the United States and Canada," photography and video of Native Americans, by Mayoke Photography
* "Tales from the Whispering Basket" Mann's first book, a compelling collection of short stories and poetry

For more information or to order a book go to:
www.whisperingbasket.com